Find Out Anything From Anyone, Anytime

Find Out Anything From Anyone, Anytime

SECRETS OF CALCULATED QUESTIONING FROM A VETERAN INTERROGATOR

James O. Pyle and Maryann Karinch

Foreword By
Gregory Hartley, coauthor
of *How to Spot a Liar*

CAREER
PRESS

Pompton Plains, N.J.

FIND OUT ANYTHING FROM ANYONE, ANYTIME
EDITED AND TYPESET BY KARA KUMPEL
Cover design by Howard Grossman/12E Design
Printed in the U.S.A.

To order this title, please call toll-free 1-800-CAREER-1 (NJ and Canada: 201-848-0310) to order using VISA or MasterCard, or for further information on books from Career Press.

The Career Press, Inc.
220 West Parkway, Unit 12
Pompton Plains, NJ 07444
www.careerpress.com

Library of Congress Cataloging-in-Publication Data
Pyle, James O., 1950-
    Find out anything from anyone, anytime : secrets of calculated questioning from a veteran interrogator / by James O. Pyle and Maryann Karinch.
        pages cm
    Includes bibliographical references and index.
    ISBN 978-1-60163-298-2 -- ISBN 978-1-60163-493-1 (ebook)
    1. Interpersonal communication. 2. Questioning. 3. Interviewing. I. Karinch, Maryann. II. Title.

BF637.C45P95 2014
158.3'9--dc23
                                                    2013040946

Dedications

JIM PYLE

To my grandpa William Owen "Stump" Bagby, who made my childhood special.

To Bob Brubaker, an old-Hollywood actor and keen salesman who made me pay attention to myself and my talents.

To Ken Hobson, a superb U.S. Army student who paid the supreme price as a soldier and intelligence professional in Tanzania in 1998.

MARYANN KARINCH

To my mother, brother, Jim, and Greg Hartley.

Acknowledgments

JIM PYLE

I want to thank Greg Hartley, a most insightful and intriguing individual and friend, for his kind Foreword, and Maryann Karinch, for expanding my concepts and understanding of good questioning and making my oral teaching presentations, concepts, and formulas a clear and interesting read. For my good wife, Deborah, who still believes in me nearly a quarter century later, and my five "natural born interrogators," Jimmy James, Corrie Anna, Sharon Marie, Jamie Dale Dorothea, and Megan

Marie Louise Pyle, for demonstrating the curiosity and discovery that I finally recaptured for myself and have delivered to you, dear reader, to consider and hopefully enhance your careers and life.

Among the band of brothers and sisters who defend this great land, I am but a stepchild. I offer my most heartfelt thanks and respect to the thousands of U.S. military, special warfare, intelligence agency, and wounded warrior students it has been my humble privilege to stand before and teach the art of Human Intelligence Collection. Thank you for your attention, your service, and your sacrifices every day and from now on.

MARYANN KARINCH

Thanks to my curious and unflappable coauthor, Jim Pyle, and the great friend and colleague who brought us together and contributed so much to this book, Greg Hartley. As always, I want to tell Jim McCormick, my mom, and my brother how much I appreciate their consistent support and helpful insights. Thank you to the other contributors to this book whom I know personally—Judith Bailey, Dr. David Sherer, Dr. Bob Domeier, Jeff Toister, Susan RoAne, Peter Earnest, and Dr. Haven Caylor and his angelic, smart, and spirited children Carter and Ammon Caylor-Brown—as well as those I don't know, but whose diligent questioning I appreciate, especially NPR's Terry Gross, Fox News's Chris Wallace, Staff Sergeant Eric Maddox, and Jamie McKenzie of From Now On. Thanks also to Colonel Harry R. Bailey (Ret.) for hosting the series of meetings Jim and I had when we launched our work together. I also greatly appreciate the support from Career Press; the team supporting us on this venture is tremendous: Adam Schwartz, Michael Pye, Kirsten Dalley, Laurie Kelly-Pye, Karen Roy, Allison Olsen, Ron Fry, Kara Kumpel, and Jeff Piasky.

Contents

Foreword

· ·

by Gregory Hartley

Throughout my business career, I have watched people interviewing new candidates or trying to resolve a problem by turning what should be a dynamic conversation into a checklist: "Do you have any...," like a game of Go Fish. I say to these people, "You are talking *at* people, not *to* them." Because business is a subset of life, there is no surprise I find people doing the same thing in their personal lives. Because of my background in human behavior, more than one of these people has asked me to write a book about information discovery to help guide their conversations with customers and others. When

Jim and I were talking about his concept for this book, I shared with him how desperately people need these skills.

When I first met Jim, he was already an interrogator in the U.S. Army's 82nd Airborne Division, returning to Monterey, California, to learn Arabic. I had not yet been trained as an interrogator. We spent most of two years there in Arabic school together, and along the way I got to know Jim well. He was among the brightest folks I met in the Army, and he had the added advantage of diverse work experiences prior to becoming an interrogator. He would constantly make observations about a person based on the words he or she chose. He would ask *why* more than any adult I had met. I assumed going to interrogation school would make me understand everything Jim had talked about.

When I left language school, it was off to interrogation school where Jim was an instructor. In interrogation school, you spend most of your time on two things: approaches, or how to get someone to "break"; and questioning, or how to get their information. Most people can get through the approaches portion of this training with lackluster performance, but questioning separates the successful interrogators from the failures. There is just no way to fake questioning; you need a logical mind, a clear plan, and a whole lot of curiosity about *what* and *why*. Without that curiosity it just turns into a checklist, or sort of a high-stakes game of Go Fish. Jim was a dynamic instructor with a spark for teaching people to think about *why* someone was saying something rather than to give a rote response and ask the next question on the list.

Jim would rely on that razor-sharp insight and a steady flow of source-driven questions to exploit the story so effectively that the questioning itself became the approach. Through many years I have watched Jim perfect his style of questioning to the point that it is his art in the interrogation room.

When I left interrogation school, I realized Jim's style was not the product of 18 weeks of training, but of a varied background overlaid with that basic skill set and used in the intelligence business and daily life. This created an understanding of how to talk *to* people in a productive manner and turn even a mundane conversation into a fluid one. There is no better person to write a book about discovery than Jim Pyle.

Jim is among the best questioning trainers in the business. He is stellar at talking *to* someone to get at the root cause of a problem, gather information about a situation, and better understand the drive of the other person in the conversation. His style of questioning will help people in all areas of life.

Expertise is the intersection of people and knowledge— knowing how to question better than the average interrogator and raising that skill to an art form isn't enough to write a book. Writing is a complex process, and getting information on paper in a form that others can understand and use is tough. When Jim asked me about writing, there was only one answer: He should partner with Maryann.

Maryann has a background as diverse as Jim's. I often say to Maryann that she should brand herself as the working-with-diverse-teams expert. She has written with and helped experts from varied backgrounds publish their thoughts and along the way picked up something from each.

Maryann and I have written seven books together about human nature and interrogation. Maryann brings not only writing and publishing savvy to the partnership, but at this point, an understanding of the concepts of interrogation and the intelligence business. Maryann was a good and quick study in the body language books we wrote together. I knew Maryann would be a strong contributing partner who would challenge Jim to think of new ways to convey his thoughts.

This book is the joint effort of these two people I know well. Maryann perfectly captures the voice of her coauthor, and I think you will find Jim's insight to human nature entertaining and useful. I hope you enjoy his way of thinking about a person's relationship to information—and how to get at that information—as much as I have.

Gregory Hartley is a decorated former U.S. Army interrogator and the coauthor of seven books on human behavior and extreme interpersonal skills. He is currently Director of Project Management for Kone Corporation.

Preface

My brother and I became interested in cars at an early age. One day, we asked our dad if he would lift up the hood so we could see what was underneath it. He grumbled a bit, but he did, and then he went back into the house. Seeing what was under the hood didn't quite satisfy us, so we started removing pieces from the car. By the time my dad discovered us, we had pulled the intake manifold off, disconnected the exhaust manifold, and broken the bolts so we could see inside the engine.

We were in so much trouble.

The positive spin on this is that we were intent on discovery, not destruction. Questioning is about discovery, and the process I've developed and taught Department of Defense students will give you the tools you need to extract all of the components from under the hood and get all the way to the pistons. You will be shocked at the depth of knowledge you will discover—if you want it—about your customers, job applicants, colleagues, vendors, and friends, as well as perfect strangers and criminals.

The first step in learning good questioning skills is grasping the true power of a question. For example, I was in line at the post office last Christmas season when a woman came in with her arms full of packages. "Wow!" I said to her, "How many friends do you have?" She volunteered that all of packages were for her daughter (and her family), who had dropped out of college to have children. She then went on to tell me how displeased she was about that choice. She and her husband had even asked the daughter to pay back the money they'd invested in her "lost" two years of college. All I did was ask a question and I got a peek under the hood at this woman's emotional engine compartment.

Placing value on questions means that, to some extent, you adopt the mentality of my students: "Interrogation never stops." In other words, the person you're posing questions to may think that the conversation has moved on past the job interview, for example, but you are still listening to every answer and discovering relevant things about the person. You may no longer be asking questions related to work history or education, but your question, "What do you think of this weather?" might lead to the knowledge that the applicant has panic attacks when she has to drive in the rain.

The secret to finding out anything you want to know is simply to ask good questions. Most people trip through life asking bad questions—of teachers, friends, coworkers, clients, prospects, experts, and suspects. Even people trained in questioning, such as journalists and lawyers, commonly ask questions that get partial or misleading answers. People in *any* profession will find immediate benefits in developing the skill and art of good questioning.

In this book, Maryann and I will explore:

✗ What's so hard about asking a good question? You've been asking questions since you could talk. The problem is that the more knowledge you acquired and the more sophisticated your vocabulary became, the worse you probably got at asking questions.

✗ Changing the way you think. The structure and flow of effective questions probably won't come naturally to you. You'll need to rewire your brain a bit, to become a little more like Socrates.

✗ Structuring a good question. Effective questioning is about accuracy and efficiency, and the way that most people structure questions on a day-to-day basis is about neither one.

✗ Using different types of questions to your advantage and knowing the difference between a good question and a bad question.

✗ Identifying discovery areas and knowing how to stick with a line of questioning that tells you all you need to know about a person, place, thing, or event in time.

✗   Honing the essential skills of listening and note-taking.

✗   Analyzing the answers you get to determine if you need more information or if the information you've been given is flawed or untrue.

✗   Using effective questioning to enable you to gain measurable advantages in your professional life and to gain real expertise *fast*.

When I was part of the interrogation world, I was known mostly as a questioning instructor and a strategic debriefer—meaning that the people around me expected me to be the best at asking questions and getting answers. I've been training other interrogators in questioning techniques since 1989. You are now the students who can exploit the questioning skills of our best interrogators and use them to your advantage in your profession.

I encourage you to see questioning as a handshake. Asking questions is an invitation to a relationship. Rather than being an aggressive or intrusive exercise—which is how some might view it—I see it as a process that enables you to connect with other people and what they want to share.

Introduction

● ●

What's So Hard About Asking a Question?

On June 23, 2013, Nik Wallenda crossed a gorge near the Grand Canyon on a two-inch wire. With no tether or safety net, he made the quarter-mile walk 1,500 feet above the ground. Millions of people watched the televised feat with wide-eyed, childlike fascination. The stunt inspired a flurry of questions from viewers: *What is he thinking? When did he start walking on wires? How does he feel? Where are his kids?* Many questions popped up in the 700,000 Tweets about #skywire; consistent with the Twitter protocol, they were concise: "Why is he wearing jeans?" and "Why did his wife let him do this?"[1]

From my perspective, Nik Wallenda's spectacular act stunned millions of people into becoming better questioners—at least for 22 minutes and 54 seconds, which is how long it took Wallenda to cross. The bursts of *what*, *when*, *why*, *where*, and *how* were the basis for a lot of well-structured, informative stories about the man and his achievement.

But complex news issues such as foreign relations, federal budgets, and trade deficits seem to invite us to ask more "sophisticated" questions—to stuff a few more syllables and concepts into our questions. For example, consider some of the questions journalists asked U.S. President Barack Obama at an April 30, 2013 press conference. The two opening questions, posed by the same person with no break allowing for an answer in between, were as follows:

> On Syria, you said that the red line was not just about chemical weapons being used but being spread, and it was a game-changer. Do you risk U.S. credibility if you don't take military action? And then on Benghazi, there are some survivors of that terror attack who say they want to come forward and testify...and they say they've been blocked. Will you allow them to testify?[2]

This pair was followed by a string of similarly flawed questions from multiple White House correspondents:

✗ By *game-changer* you mean U.S. military action?[3]

✗ Will you help them come forward and just say it once and for all?[4]

✗ A senior member of the Armed Services Committee has said that Benghazi and Boston are both examples of the U.S. going backwards on national security. Is he right? And did our intelligence miss something?[5]

✗ Are you getting all the intelligence and information you need from the Russians? And should Americans be worried when they go to big, public events now?[6]

✗ Do you still have the juice to get the rest of your agenda through this Congress?[7]

Note that this is the exact sequence of the questions. So in the first nine questions posed to the President—and this is about halfway into the press conference—what are the only words President Obama would have needed to answer each of these questions? "Yes" and "no." He did not give yes-or-no answers, of course; he talked at length about the issues raised. This is why some people who watched the press conference may have concluded that the journalists did a marvelous job of drawing out information from the President. In reality, the journalists with substandard questions merely benefited from the fact that President Obama had a great many points he intended to make during the press conference.

The paradox of questioning is that simple questions can lead to detailed, on-target answers, but complicated questions get you single-word answers from a subject who doesn't want to talk, and unrestrained answers from a person who does. In this book, I will teach you the process of skillfully asking simple questions to extract the information you need, regardless of the type of subject.

The questioning techniques exposed and explored in this book come from the world of Human Intelligence

Collection through interrogation, interviewing, and debriefing. Interrogation is a science because there are specific scientific techniques to follow and model. It is an art because, in a real sense, it is theater for one. It is also a discipline in that it follows a system of organization.

Questioning is the foundation for effective interrogation; it is the central component of the discipline of interrogation. At the same time, in learning questioning, it's important that you separate it from the any preconceived notions you have about interrogation. The questioning process you will learn in this book has nothing to do with coercion, intimidation, or any other techniques associated with uncooperative sources. The process of questioning I teach can turn someone who is only marginally cooperative into someone more willing to talk, but it is not designed to convert a hostile source into a friendly one.

As you begin learning the process, consider this good news: We're all are all natural born questioners! From the time we start uttering real words, we ask, "Why?" and every other interrogative. It's human nature for kids to try to verify and validate every day. In learning how to question effectively as an adult, you need to recapture that persistent and unbiased curiosity of your youth.

But it's more than recapturing that childlike curiosity. It's a matter of focus. When kids ask a question, they want to know one thing. They point to a bug they've never seen before and ask, "What's that?" As adults, our biggest downfall in questioning is that we try to get too much information at one time. Adults point to a bug and ramble on: "Look at that strange bug. I've never seen anything like it before. Where did it come from? Do you know if it bites? Do you suppose it will eat my tomatoes?"

So a foundational lesson in the questioning process you will learn in this book is this: **Find out one thing at a time.** The alternative is finding out a lot of information that you have to sort through in order to get the facts you really need. And that's the downfall of the White House correspondents.

ORIGINS OF THE
QUESTIONING PROCESS

Fort Huachuca, which is in Arizona about 15 miles north of the border with Mexico, is home to the United States Army Intelligence Center and School. It's where I began my career as an interrogator, human intelligence collector, and later, a military instructor for Department of Defense interrogators and strategic debriefers.

In the mid-1980s, the interrogation course at Ft. Huachuca was a mere nine weeks, which is short if you consider the breadth of skills interrogators need to perform effectively in the field. Classes on interrogation approaches, cross-cultural communications, and a number of other interpersonal skills ran back-to-back. The course was linked to the language training program at the Defense Language Institute in Monterey, California. The concept was to absorb a defense-critical foreign language in a condensed period of time and then bring it into the interrogation course and apply it as needed.

Questioning training was a critical component for effective and efficient interrogation. It was a five-day block of instruction, eight hours a day, or a total of 40 hours of instruction. It took the students from question #1 to the last question they could ever possibly ask in areas of military-related questioning such as missions, logistics, and personnel. Slide after slide—there were hundreds— listed an exact sequence of questions for each area. It was mind-numbing to the extent that no one wanted to teach it.

My grandfather had always told me, "You get the job nobody else wants and you'll always have job security," so I volunteered to teach the questioning block. I hated it too, but found a way to put the experience to good use when I left the Army.

A company called Phoenix Consulting Group was just starting up and had secured a contract from the Defense Intelligence Agency (DIA) to teach interrogation courses. Prior to that, the Army and Marine Corps had been the only entities offering such courses for military and intelligence personnel. Phoenix remained the only certified non-military source of such training for the next six years until the company was acquired and systematically dismantled by another organization. When Phoenix hired me, we were under United States Senate supervision and had the distinction of our students never being associated with any of interrogation scandals like Abu Ghraib that shook public trust in military interrogation practices.

The program of instruction I developed at Phoenix of course included questioning. Not the boring version that forced students to memorize a series of questions in a precise order, but the kind that you will learn in this book. I developed an effective process of questioning that does have rules and structure, but not rigid rules and structure. It engages your intellect and personality in the process.

Good questioning is not about knowing what questions to ask, but how to ask questions the right way. You will know which ones to ask by understanding and employing my formula for questioning.

WHAT'S IN IT FOR YOU?

The first class we taught through Phoenix Consulting Group was of Navy SEALs, and we went onsite to teach it in a bunker on the Pacific Ocean. These may have been the best group of students I've ever experienced. They were hungry to learn everything I knew so they would make no mistakes when lives were at stake.

My guess is that you have a laser-like focus analogous to theirs and that's why you're going to be a great student. Your probably aren't in life-or-death situations like the SEALs, but you have a distinct purpose for wanting to know how to question well. You want this skill set so you can achieve something that's important to you.

What you are about to learn is how to:

✗ Identify and practice good questioning techniques.

✗ Recognize types of questions to avoid.

✗ Know the questions required when hearing unconfirmed reports or gossip.

✗ Practice good listening techniques and exploit all leads.

✗ Identify questioning models.

✗ Determine when and how to control the conversation.

Gaining these skills will give you an advantage in whatever you do—sales, law, law enforcement, parenting, customer service, human resources, medicine, counseling, teaching, negotiating, journalism, and more. The list is endless. You wouldn't be asking questions right now unless you needed to have answers. The skills of questioning help you get complete answers faster.

Questioning is one of the interpersonal skills that delivers instant gratification: You ask a question; you get an answer. In addition to that, the long-term benefits of learning a questioning discipline are these:

✗   Your rapport-building skills take on another dimension. Good questioning relies on rapport to some extent, but knowing how and when to ask questions also goes a long way to enhancing your rapport with another person. **Questioning well is a skill that helps you get closer to people. It can be a warm, interactive process, even if you have an agenda.**

✗   You learn to use active listening techniques habitually. In the way interrogators use it, active listening involves both demonstration and perception. You indicate through words and body language that you are engaged in what the other person is saying; at the same time, you are listening for subtext and observing behavior.

✗   Your critical thinking skills sharpen. Your well-ordered construction of questions is a workout for your cognitive processes. Instead of spewing questions that are tinged with emotion and/or expressing a collection of random thoughts, you take a refined approach. As a matter of habit, the structure of your questions and your word choices reflect discipline. Your critical thinking also develops through looking for holes in answers, hearing what extraneous bits have been planted in them, and planning the next question.

✗ You have one more screwdriver in the toolkit that gives you a competitive advantage. If you're in sales, your toolkit might already include in-depth product knowledge, charisma, and a well-respected company backing you up. Add questioning skills to that and the odds of closing deals shift even more in your favor. If you're a parent—let's say of teenagers—your "competitive advantage" might be discovering all the facts about something they'd like to cover up. I know what it's like to have to teenagers and I would never say that I used my questioning expertise *against* them; I used it to help protect them. One of my grown daughters told me recently, "I know I wasn't easy, but I would have been harder to raise if you hadn't stayed a step ahead of me."

An offshoot of all of the benefits of cultivating questioning skills is a deeper understanding of why people are willing to answer your questions. It's valuable to look at these reasons because, if someone is giving you answers but none of these descriptions of motivation seem to fit, ask yourself if the person might be making up a story.

✗ The subject is naturally inclined to divulge information. When most people hear a phone ring, the tendency is to answer it. Similarly, a good many people hear a question and immediately want to answer it. Every day on the MSN.com home page, there is a survey question about a current news item. The basic question, tweaked to reflect the day's news is, "What do you think of..." Within a couple of hours or less, you might see 250,000 responses! As a skilled questioner, you will be able to sail through a session with someone who can't resist responding to the daily poll. You will need to stay disciplined, however, because people who are comfortable with giving up a lot of information have the potential to take you off course.

✗   The subject stands to benefit by giving you information. In a sales situation, a serious buyer has compelling reasons to tell you the whole truth. You ask the questions to determine the must-haves and the other factors that would please the customer; the customer answers the questions so she can get what she wants. The disconnect in the scenario is that you may not have what she seems to wants, so your next set of questions may have to be "what else" questions until she hits on features of your product.

✗   The subject stands to lose something by not giving you information. Physicians in an acute care position have a distinct advantage as questioners: If the subject doesn't deliver truthful and complete answers, dire consequences might result. There are many situations in which this relationship isn't quite as drastic, of course. Parents who issue the dangling ultimatum, "Tell me what happened—or else!" suggest that confessing will involve a lot less pain than hiding the facts.

✗ The subject feels as though he owes you something and information might repay the debt. This can be part of a quid pro quo exchange in which you give a little information about yourself to make the other person feel obligated or more comfortable to give a little information about himself. Or, it might be that you did someone a favor and the person literally feels indebted to you, so when you ask a question, he feels it's his duty to answer it.

A friend told me a story that illustrates why someone who lacks all of these motivations would answer questions. She had become so irritated by daily robo-calls from politicians and political parties in the run-up to a major election that she decided to participate in one of the non-robotic calls. For the most part, she gave the pollster truly odd responses—a.k.a. lies. So if you're in a sales, legal, or other situation in which you start to suspect the person really has no motivation to talk to you, start looking for signs that the information isn't credible.

ONE THING AT A TIME

Earlier in the chapter, I noted that a foundational lesson in the questioning process I teach is to **find out one thing at a time**. This is a tenet to carry forward as you go through the book. Focusing on one thing at a time may not sound like a mentally challenging task, but consider some common ways we fail to achieve it:

✗   A mother asks her second-semester college fresh-man, "What happens when you finish the term and come home and can't get a job?" She gets frustrated when he responds, "We have a few days to kinda wrap up the semester—you know, some parties and cleaning up the dorm—and then I'll head back. But you know, I've been working on my resume and got some contacts through Facebook." He didn't pay much attention past "What happens when you finish..." In Mom's mind, she asked, "What will you do if you can't get a job this summer?" so his answer seems evasive. She thinks she stuck to the one-thing-at-a-time rule, but what came out of her mouth did not.

✗   A police officer asks, "Why didn't you slow down as you came around the corner into the school zone?" The driver responds, "Of course I slowed down. If you don't slow down around that corner, you'd go flying into the guard rail." The officer thought he asked why the motorist didn't slow down as he entered the school zone. If he had, the question would have been, "Why didn't you slow down as you came into the school zone?"

Now think back to the beginning of the chapter and the questions related to Nik Wallenda versus the questions on policy issues posed by journalists at a press conference. The distinctions between good and bad questions should be starting to take shape. A key distinction is that simple questions such as "Why is he wearing jeans?" have two important qualities: They require a narrative response and focus on a single issue.

So, if you stop here and remember everything you learned, you're about 10 percent better at questioning than you were when you started reading. Let's go for the other 90 percent!

Chapter 1
Changing the Way You Think

I know you won't believe me but the highest form of human excellence is to question oneself and others.

—Socrates

What do you know that I don't know, that I wouldn't know if I didn't ask?

—Jim Pyle

"Changing the way you think" has a number of different meanings in the context of learning to excel in the art of questioning. The structure and flow of effective questions probably won't come naturally to you. You will rewire your brain a bit as you refine the art. The most important change is to make questioning a discovery, to see it as an expression of open-minded curiosity.

Some people hesitate to ask questions because they see it as probing or prying, an intrusive act that makes others uncomfortable. In reality, questioning should be the opposite. It is a way to show other people you are interested in them; it's more like a handshake than a poke in the ribs.

When I was 19 years old, I started Bible College and became a preacher. For seven years, I gave the congregation all kinds of answers to their problems and never asked them a single question. When I realized all I did for a living was push information at people—and get paid almost nothing for it—I decided to change professions. I got a job that involved as much questioning and listening as it did talking, and it turned out to be a dream come true: I sold cemetery plots. This was no ordinary cemetery, though. It was Forest Lawn Memorial Park, which at the time was the perpetual home of Humphrey Bogart, Nat King Cole, Walt Disney, W.C. Fields, and Clark Gable, among other celebrities. (Elizabeth Taylor and Michael Jackson have since joined them.)

I went door to door and asked a lot of questions: How much is peace of mind worth to you? What would your wife do if you suddenly passed on? What is stopping you from making the decision right now? In answering questions like these, people invited me into their lives. I learned more about their family life, values, fears, health, and finances than I ever knew about most of the people I preached to in the years prior. Forest Lawn Memorial Park represented human connections to me, as well as a substantial increase in income. It turned out that asking the right questions was rewarding on at least two levels.

FOCUS ON DISCOVERY

As part of developing this book, I engaged in series of exchanges with a woman named Judith, whom I had just met.[1] These conversations set the stage for learning the first rules of good questioning. They also spotlight why you need to change the way you think to hone your questioning skills.

Judith had no exposure to my questioning process prior to our exchanges. Going into the session, she didn't even know as much as you know now, which is the importance of focusing on only one thing at a time. In my first conversation with Judith I was trying to get driving directions to a place I'd never been. To make it more challenging, she does not drive a car, nor has she even tried to do so in the past 25 years because of a depth-perception problem. (At least she has a legitimate excuse for having had eight minor accidents during her driver's education class.)

Judith has a limited sense of cardinal directions (north, south, east, and west), and relies on a combination of buses and light rail to get where she needs to go, so her awareness of street names between Point A and Point B is minimal. I wanted to see if my questioning could lead to my own understanding of how to drive from her home to a destination that was unknown to me. I asked questions such as, "What is the route you take to get from here to the bus stop?" and "How long does it take you to walk from your house to the bus stop?" I asked, "What do you see out the window of the bus?" and "What else do you see?" From these questions, I was able to piece together driving directions, segment by segment, up to the final segment of the journey. In that final segment, from the above-ground rail, Judith walks through a residential area to the location. It's a footpath, so it's not the way a driver would be able to go. Asking her what she would see in front her, to the left, right, and behind when she arrived at the destination did provide the necessary information to determine how a car would access the property. It wasn't perfect, but the 360-degree view gave me enough clues to find the location.

Questions such as "What do you see where you are now?" encourage the subject to envision key locations as though she were making the trip at the moment. In questioning for directions, you want to see what that person sees; you use that person's eyes.

Now imagine you're doing the same exercise with someone who doesn't know cardinal directions, speaks a different language (so you're relying on an interpreter), and walks wherever he needs to go—and what he knows could help you save lives. That's what a battlefield interrogator might face.

SOCRATES AND YOU

The point of an exchange such as the one I had with Judith-the-non-driver is to prove that it is possible for good questioning to yield the information you need from a source who doesn't even realize she has anything worthwhile to contribute. For example, good questioning of people in the vicinity of an accident or a crime sometimes turns passersby who think they know nothing into key witnesses.

Michael Dobson, author of the book *Creative Project Management*, blogged about just such a situation that had happened to him:

> Today, Tuesday, April 13, 2010, is the 35th anniversary of a killing spree in Wheaton, Maryland. My girlfriend and I were on our way home from *Young Frankenstein* when we drove right through the middle of it.
>
> Michael Edward Pearch shot seven people, all African-American, killing two and wounding the rest. There were indications, police said, that the shooting was racially motivated. All the victims were black and the gunman was white. He passed up at least one car with whites, said police, as he walked down a highway looking for another target.
>
> There were at least two such cars. One of them was mine.
>
> Pearch, an unemployed carpenter living with his mother in Silver Spring, Maryland, left home about 7:30 p.m. on Sunday, April 13, 1975, and drove to the nearby Wheaton Plaza shopping mall. He was wearing his Army fatigues, a knapsack with 250 rounds of ammunition, and a machete strapped to his chest. He carried a .45 caliber [semi-]automatic pistol.

He walked to the traffic light at the entrance to the mall, where he shot and killed [one man, wounded his wife, and fired at another man].

The panic started at once. "Some witnesses ducked for cover. Others just stood there and watched in disbelieving shock," said police captain Miles Daniels. One particularly brave man called the police and began following the gunman.

We were on our way home from the movies. It was a warm spring evening. The car windows were open. As I neared the intersection of Georgia Avenue and University Boulevard (a major intersection), I heard what I thought at first were gunshots.

But gunshots on a lazy Sunday evening on a busy suburban street? Surely, I must be imagining things. Then I saw the man who had followed the gunman. He was ducking behind cars. Well, if there wasn't any gunfire, then surely the man was just playing some sort of game.

The light turned green. I pulled forward. As I reached the intersection, I saw two men in the left turn lane on the other side of the street. One man was standing. He was white. One man was face down. He was black. In his right hand, he was carrying a brown paper bag.

If there wasn't any gunfire, and the man ducking behind cars was playing some sort of game, then I figured I was looking at some drunks, with one of them (clutching his booze in a brown paper bag) passed out in the street.

As I drove through the intersection, I passed within five feet of Michael Edward Pearch, the shooter, and his most recent victim....

There was a police station about a mile north of the intersection, right on our way home, so I pulled in. "There's a drunk passed out in the left turn lane at Georgia and University," I told the officer at the desk.

"Wait here," the officer said.

Moments later three plainclothes officers came out of the back room. "Are those the eyewitnesses to the murders?" one of the officers asked.

It was not until that moment that I had any idea what I had seen.

We spent the rest of the evening in a room with an increasing number of witnesses. It wasn't until afterward that I learned the rest of the story.[2]

At the time Dobson watched incidents unfold from his car, he had no idea he was collecting pertinent information for a murder investigation. Most of us have experiences like this on a less dramatic level, and when someone asks the right questions, he extracts that information from us and puts it to use. It could be something as simple as knowing where the capers are shelved in the grocery store; you may never have bought capers, but you've passed by them so many times you know where they are when someone asks.

This is the approach that Socrates famously took in Plato's dialogue *Meno* regarding the slave boy who had never studied geometry but was able to solve a complex geometry problem simply by responding to Socrates' series of questions. In this part of the conversation Socrates explains to Meno how the boy who knew no geometry could accomplish such a feat. It perfectly illustrates the Socratic Method—and gives you one more good reason to learn how to question well.

SOCRATES: What do you think, Meno? Has he answered with any opinions that were not his own?

MENO: No, they were all his.

SOCRATES: Yet he did not know, as we agreed a few minutes ago.

MENO: True.

SOCRATES: But these opinions were somewhere in him, were they not?

MENO: Yes.

SOCRATES: So a man who does not know has in himself true opinions on a subject without having knowledge.

MENO: It would appear so.

SOCRATES: At present these opinions, being newly aroused, have a dream-like quality. But if the same questions are put to him on many occasions and in different ways, you can see that in the end he will have a knowledge on the subject as accurate as anybody's.

MENO: Probably.

SOCRATES: This knowledge will not come from teaching but from questioning. He will recover it for himself.

QUIZZING THE KNOW-IT-ALL

A reverse exercise to the one I did with Judith on directions is having someone who knows nothing about a subject question someone who's an expert. Judith kindly served as the interrogator and came into the process with no training in questioning and almost no knowledge of the subject, which was car racing. Her questions reflect the kind of structure common to someone who wants to build rapport, but has no idea how to do that while concurrently extracting the information she wants. In this case, her secret objective (which she documented without my knowledge) was to discover how I felt about Danica Patrick as a professional driver. Maryann simply instructed Judith to move into a conversation about race-car driving in a comfortable way and then subtly find out what I thought of Patrick.

Her opening question was perfect: "How long have you been a fan of racing?"

"50 years."

Her second question is typical for a journalist, for example, who may not know anything about the subject matter, but wants to seem informed: "So, do you like NASCAR rather than drag racing, or something else?" The flaw in the question is that it suggests an answer and it doesn't follow the one-thing-at-a-time rule. A better question would be: "What kind of racing is your favorite?" As I go through this real scenario, consider that this untrained questioner is a very bright person who listens to news interview programs, stays on top of Presidential press conferences, and has unusual gifts at rapport-building. All of that aside, she loses ground almost immediately by asking a bad question.

I responded, "I've never been to a drag race, but I've been to lots of NASCAR races."

"And do you travel around—mostly around here or go places like the Indianapolis 500?" Again, the question addresses more than one area of the topic, but that's not its only problem. As is typical for journalists, for example, who want to demonstrate they know something about a subject about which they know very little, Judith has thrown in the name of the only race she knows. As you listen to news interview shows, pay attention to name dropping like this. It suggests to the undiscerning listener that the journalist probably has a handle—at least somewhat—on the topic of discussion, but in fact it may show that the person really has no idea about the subject area. In short, it's better to say less in the question than more.

"Last weekend, I just came back from the Indianapolis 500, which is not a NASCAR race. It is an open-wheel style car. NASCAR is a full-bodied car. But I've done both over the years."

Her next question was almost on target: "Do drivers who do NASCAR also do the Indianapolis 500, although that's a slightly different class?" A better question, which would have inched her closer to getting the information she wanted, would have been: "What NASCAR drivers also drive at the Indianapolis 500?"

My answer to her question still allowed her to pursue the path of finding out how I felt about Danica Patrick, but the exchange was protracted. In response to "do they do both," I said, "They used to."

Had she asked the "what" question, I probably would have said, "None, but there are some drivers who have done both." That statement would have logically provoked the question, "Who are they?" One of the answers is "Danica Patrick." With that response, she had a clean opening to ask me how I felt about Danica Patrick as a driver.

The take-aways from this unschooled, spontaneous exchange are primarily:

1. Most of Judith's questions throughout the entire 20-minute interview were yes/no questions: "Do you travel around...?" and "Do drivers...?" I gave a narrative response, but strictly speaking, I could have just said yes or no, just as President Obama could have given yes-or-no answers in the press conference referenced in the Introduction. In a situation in which a suspect or adultcrous spouse is responding to questions that could incriminate him or her, this style of questioning is completely ineffectual.

2. By not using interrogatives for most of the interaction, a great deal of extraneous information—I've spared you the full conversation—entered into the exchange. Rapport-building was certainly occurring, but it is possible to build rapport and still

drive toward the information you need. About 80 percent of the conversation involved extraneous information. (The use of interrogatives is covered thoroughly in Chapter 2.)

INTRODUCTORY EXERCISES

Judith stuck with me as I took her through three introductory exercises designed to sensitize someone to the elements of good questioning. These exercises help you change the way you think about questioning, step by step.

"Be a kid again," I told her. "It's all about discovery." I asked her to go back in time to when she was about 2 and approach the entire exercise with that mentality. And then I showed her a picture:

"Who's that?" she asked.

"That's Santa Claus. And he's coming to your house."

"Why is he coming to my house?"

"To bring you something."

"What will he bring?

"Toys. But he's only coming on one special night."

"When is he coming?"

"Christmas Eve. And not only is he coming to your house, he's going to all the houses where children live all over the world—all in one night!"

"How can he do that?"

I begin classes with interrogators with the Santa Claus scenario. The very sight of the jolly fat man brings out the kid in almost everyone. I can't think of anyone who genuinely committed to a 2-year-old mentality who deviated from good questions in the Santa Claus exchange. In her role as a 2-year-old, Judith automatically switched from a "Do you think..." and "Would you say..." style of questioning to complete commitment to simple, focused questions.

The second exercise begins like this: "What's the most important thing about the TV game show *Jeopardy*?" And then we play a little *Jeopardy*. The obvious point is that everything is stated in the form of a question, beginning with an interrogative, or you lose. For example, here's a winner:

Alex Trebek reads the answer: "Two of the four Shakespeare plays in which ghosts appear on stage."

Ken Jennings' written response is "What are *Hamlet* and *Richard III*?"[3]

And here's a loser:

"The answer is, 'Selected some material from a larger work.'"

Wolf Blitzer's non-question response, which was incorrect no matter how it was phrased, was, "Annotated."

Alex Trebek replied, "Wolf, things have not worked out as you had hoped for, I'm sure."[4]

The third introductory exercise is to explore a subject with which the questioner is unfamiliar, using only simple, one-topic questions that begin with *who, what, when, where,* or *why*. With Judith, we chose the topic of being a DJ—that is, playing recorded music for an audience and inserting entertaining commentary as the opportunity arises. This is one of my favorite exercises. Judith began her questioning as follows:

JUDITH: "What did you like about DJ-ing?"

JAMES: "I liked getting paid to play music and drink beer."

JUDITH: "What was your favorite music?"

JAMES: "One kind I liked to play was classic rock 'n' roll."

Here I gave her an opening to ask a very important question. I said, "One kind I liked..." Whether or not the respondent gives that kind of obvious opening to probe, the next question should be, "What else?" It is difficult to develop the listening aptitude to know when to ask "what else" as well as the discipline to ask it. The rule of thumb is, if you ask a question and get an answer that suggests there might be additional information, ask that question again. So, "What's your favorite music?" gets a particular answer, and "What else do you like a lot?" is a tightly related question that probes more deeply.

"Who hires you to DJ?" might get a response such as "brides and grooms." "Who else hires you to DJ?" pulls out at least one more bit of information.

I'm going to leave the DJ scenario briefly to give proper emphasis to the importance of asking "what else?" Ask a child what she had for lunch and she might say, "a sandwich." A typical follow-up question from an adult would be, "What kind of sandwich?" But the next question in an effective questioning scheme would actually be, "What else did you have for lunch?" You find out she had milk, peaches, and a cookie in addition to the sandwich. *Then* you ask, "What kind of sandwich?" If you didn't use that sequence, you may never find out what else the little girl had for lunch because undisciplined questioning follows the bouncing ball. The lesson is this: Stay with that one question and make sure it's answered before moving on to the particulars.

In a business context the sandwich question might play out like this:

Ineffective

TECHNICIAN: What problem are you having with the software?

CUSTOMER: It won't let me resize images.

TECHNICIAN: What kind of images?

That conversation leads them down a path of discussing images and the reasons why they can't be resized, or how they might be resized. Contrast that exchange with the following one in terms of what it means to the flow of conversation and, ultimately, the customer's sense that the company is really trying to help him.

Effective

TECHNICIAN: What problem are you having with the software?

CUSTOMER: It won't let me resize images.

TECHNICIAN: What other problems are you having with the software?

CUSTOMER: It won't let me export images to another program, and it freezes when I try to re-color an image.

TECHNICIAN: Any other problems?

CUSTOMER: That's it.

At that point, the technician has a package of facts that happen to be interrelated, and he has a firm grasp of how to help the customer. This is the difference between aimless dribbling and passing the ball so your team can score.

Let's use an example from enemy interrogation to make it clear how this works in a life-and death situation:

INTERROGATOR: What were you doing?

PRISONER: Placing an IED.

An unseasoned interrogator would then ask, "Where?" But a better tack would be, "What else were you doing?"

PRISONER: Surveillance.

INTERROGATOR: What else?

PRISONER: That's all.

After discovering that the prisoner was doing just two things, then it's time to ferret out the details of the IED and the nature of the surveillance activities.

At some point the "what else" questions lead the person to say, "That's it. Can't think of any more." Then you know you're done with that line of questioning and can move on.

Returning to the DJ scenario, Judith then asked, "What kind of rock 'n' roll do you consider classic?"

JAMES: I'll do it by years: '50s, '60s, '70s, '80s, and '90s.

JUDITH: Which style is your favorite?

JAMES: I have a favorite in each decade.

JUDITH: If you look at your favorite from each decade, what similarities do they have? Is there something common to all of your favorites?

That question was excellent. It belongs in the mix and is exactly the kind of imaginative question that can trigger a spontaneous response. So, I'm not suggesting it be eliminated because it doesn't follow a prescribed flow or structure; I'm just suggesting that the placement of it needs to be carefully considered.

For now, just consider that Judith's question was designed to draw out psychological information about me, not just facts. The power of a well-structured question like that cannot be underestimated.

Psychological questions can take someone off guard so much that what follows is thinking, and in this case, trying to remember particular songs and what they might have in common. No easy or prepared answers readily came to mind. Alternatively, the lack of response could signal that the subject was making the whole story up and just hadn't prepared the part of the lie that addresses that question. This is a topic explored in greater depth in Chapter 6.

✗ ✗ ✗

In the Introduction you learned to find out one thing at a time. Add to that foundational lesson the importance of viewing questioning as discovery, and the two key coaching points in this chapter are:

1. In general, ask for a narrative response, rather than *yes* or *no*. An obvious exception is "Will you marry me?"

2. Know when to ask, "What else?"

To do both of these things well, you probably need to fight your impulses. By learning how to question well, you are starting to change the way you think.

Chapter 2

. . . .

The Structure of a Good Question

Effective questioning is about accuracy and efficiency. To the lessons I've already provided, I am going to add a couple more on how to begin a question, the importance of excising bias from your questioning, and how long to make a question.

USING INTERROGATIVES

A good question should always start with an interrogative. People commonly fail to use this most basic structural element of a good question—*who, what, where, when, how,* or *why.* Openers tend to be "Do you..." and "Could you..." which elicit no more than a "Yes" or a "No." On the other hand, narrative responses elicited by an interrogative are rich with additional information and leads.

Briefly, here is the difference, in relation to the accuracy and efficiency of collecting information:

A well-structured exchange would look like this:

> *What did you do last night?*
>
> I went to the theater.
>
> *What else?*
>
> Just that.
>
> *What theater did you go to last night?*
>
> The Fox Theater.
>
> *Where is the Fox?*
>
> Downtown Denver, across from the convention center.
>
> *What did you see?*
>
> A revival of *Equus.*

In contrast, these questions lead nowhere:

> *Did you do something last night?*
>
> Yes.
>
> *Go anywhere?*
>
> Went downtown.
>
> *Just to hang out?*
>
> No. Had tickets to the theater.

Was it a good show?

Yes.

You might think I should stop the discussion right here. After all, you may assume there aren't many things can you say about using interrogatives except, "Start your questions with them." Actually, the discussion is just beginning, because the proper use of interrogatives means that the questioner is demonstrating curiosity without prejudice. Using other questioning forms, as well as using interrogatives followed by certain qualifying information, reflects curiosity with prejudice and perhaps even an agenda, such as the kind that hosts of so-called news interview programs have with guests of an opposite political leaning.

I can hear the protests from where I'm sitting. You are thinking back to some of the great interviewers and their questioning style and ready to fight me on the rule of interrogatives—because those great questioners violated it frequently. Mike Wallace was one of the top television interrogators of all time during his years on *60 Minutes,* and even prior that 40-year stint. He had a reputation for aggressive questioning and was notorious for, among other things, bringing Barbra Streisand to tears and angering the Ayatollah Khomeini to the point where he ordered the assassination of Egyptian President Anwar Sadat. Although the narratives he wrapped around direct questioning were typically tinged with a distinct point of view, his questions were primarily rather neutral. He tended to rely on interrogatives and ask short, pointed questions that drove people into a corner. There is no inherent prejudice in questions such as the following, yet they all provoked an animated response from the interviewee:

- To novelist Ayn Rand, founder of Objectivism: "What is Randism?"[1]

✗ To then–presidential candidate Ronald Reagan: "How many blacks are there on your top campaign staff, Governor?"[2]

✗ To entertainer Barbra Streisand: "Why are you so attackable?" and "When are you going to be 50?"[3]

✗ To former First Lady Nancy Reagan: "What was your husband's role in Iran-Contra?"[4]

Mike Wallace was an interrogator, and many of the people he interviewed probably felt as though they were detainees at Guantanamo Bay. In contrast, Mike Wallace's son Chris, an Emmy-award-winning journalist and host of the program *Fox News Sunday*, is squarely focused on discovery and discussion. In fact, his style exemplifies discovery questioning. Growing up, Chris Wallace did not have his father as a professional role model. His stepfather, future CBS News President Bill Leonard, was the one who introduced young Chris to journalism by hiring him to help Walter Cronkite at the 1964 Republican National Convention; he was just 16 years old.

Chris Wallace is a master of what I call the journalistic *double-dip*. He asks good questions, although they might come in pairs; that is, he double dips, perhaps often not knowing if he will get a chance to ask the person another question after she answers the first one. (This is distinct from a compound question, which I describe in Chapter 3 as one of the "bad" types of questions.)

There is also a lighter side to the discussion of using interrogatives. In reviewing a number of David Letterman interviews, I listened for questions beginning with one of the key words. In interview after interview, it was often the banter that led to comments from the guest rather than Letterman's questions. And then Maryann singled out an interview that Letterman did with Sasha Baron Cohen in character. He came on the *Late Show* in 2006 as Borat, the titular character from his movie *Borat: Cultural Learnings of America for Make Benefit Glorious Nation of Kazakhstan.* Perhaps not surprisingly, when Letterman shifted into the persona of someone interviewing a "head of state," between laughter and wincing, he took a different approach to questioning:

✗   What do we need to know about you?

✗   What should we know about Kazakhstan?

✗   What have you learned about the United States as you've traveled around the country?

✗   What are we going to see in the clip, Borat? [He asked this question as part of the introduction to the segment of the movie played on the show, which was about driving lessons in America.]

✗   What state are you in when you this was filmed?[5]

David Letterman is an entertainer, not a journalist, but when he wore the mantle of a journalist in his interview with Borat, he transformed himself into a good questioner.

In the following subsection, consider my assertion that interrogatives used well lead to unbiased questions, whereas others contain bias and perhaps reflect an agenda.

Consider also how straightforward, unbiased questions introduced with an interrogative can come across like daggers—á la Mike Wallace—in contrast to blunt-edged, meandering questions that are actually intended to attack the interviewee and/or manifest a point of view.

CURIOSITY WITH PREJUDICE

In the opening of Chapter 1, I urged you to see questioning as discovery, defined as the expression of open-minded curiosity. That means curiosity without prejudice. You will find yourself automatically turning to interrogatives to begin questions when you consciously avert bias, and largely turning away from them when your judgment about the other person or the topic at hand colors your questioning. Some of the most renowned interviewers of our era illustrate this point.

National Public Radio's Terry Gross, host of *Fresh Air*, has been justifiably lauded for her astute interviews, which are a product of meticulous research and seemingly genuine interest in her guests. If there is bias, it tends to be favorable bias, which supports rapport-building with the guest.

Her May 2013 interview with novelist Stephen King began with a question about his latest book, a crime novel: "What do you like about that genre as a reader and as a writer?" That was followed by a string of *why*, *what*, and *who* questions that led to colorful insights on the novel.[6]

Not all of her interviews took that course, however, and one of the most notorious was with Gene Simmons, lead vocalist of the rock bank KISS. Following a rocky beginning—Simmons criticized her mispronunciation of his Hebrew birth name—the interview quickly became a contentious encounter. In contrast with the Stephen King interview, Gross started out with three "did you" questions. It's more the style of a prosecutor interrogating a witness than a talk show host interviewing a guest. As the interview progressed, she nearly abandoned interrogatives and asked questions that played into Simmons's confrontational modus operandi:

> TERRY GROSS: Are you trying to say to me that all that matters to you is money?

> GENE SIMMONS: I will contend, and you try to disprove it, that the most important thing as we know it on this planet, in this plane, is, in fact, money. Want me to prove it?

> TERRY GROSS: Well, let's cut to the chase. How much—how much money do you have?

> GENE SIMMONS: Gee, a lot more than NPR.

> TERRY GROSS: Oh, I know. I—you're very defensive on money, aren't you?

> GENE SIMMONS: No, I'm not, I'm just trying to show you that there's a big world out there, and reading books is wonderful. I've certainly read, well, perhaps as many as you have, but there's a delusional kind of notion that runs rampant in—

> TERRY GROSS: Wait, wait, could we just get something straight?

> GENE SIMMONS: Of course.

TERRY GROSS: I'm not here to prove that I'm smart—

GENE SIMMONS: Not you—

TERRY GROSS: I'm not here to prove that you're not smart or that you don't read books or can't make a lot of money—

GENE SIMMONS: This is not about you. You're being very defensive—why are you doing that?

TERRY GROSS: [*laughs*] It's contagious.

GENE SIMMONS: Yeah.

TERRY GROSS: Can we get back to your make-up? What do you use to paint your face, and do you ever break out from that?

GENE SIMMONS: No, it's actually oil-based. It's Stein's makeup...is one of the brand names, but you can use lots of different...lots of things. I don't think I've ever been asked that question. But no. My skin is more beautiful than yours.

TERRY GROSS: Let's get to the studded codpiece.

GENE SIMMONS: Oh yes.

TERRY GROSS: Do you have a sense of humor about that?

GENE SIMMONS: No.

TERRY GROSS: Does that seem funny to you? Are you—

GENE SIMMONS: No, it holds in my manhood.

TERRY GROSS: [*laughs*] That's right.

GENE SIMMONS: Otherwise it would be too much for you to take. You'd have to put the book down and confront life. The notion is that if you want to welcome me with open arms, I'm afraid you're also going to have to welcome me with open legs.

TERRY GROSS: That's a really obnoxious thing to say.

GENE SIMMONS: No it's not, it's being—why should I say something behind your back that I can't tell you to your face?

TERRY GROSS: Wait, it—it—has it come to this? Is this the only way that you can talk to a woman? To do that shtick?[7]

When I was first exposed to this interview, all Maryann did was read Terry Gross's questions in the first half of the interview; she did not offer any of Gene Simmons's answers. Standing alone, the questions seemed dysfunctional and aggressive to me. They suggested that she was coming at him rather than wanting something from him. There was very little sense of discovery as I've defined it. In all fairness, of course, a normal human response to being criticized at the outset would be to proceed with some bias—but the point is not whether or not Gross had a normal human response. I'm simply using this exchange to point out how prejudice infects and degrades questioning.

But being the professional she is, Terry Gross turned it around before the interview was over. It's as though she hit a reset button. After a Simmons rant on the boring nature of NPR, she returned the discussion to KISS and even created an opening for him to talk respectfully about his mother. Her next string of questions relied primarily on interrogatives:

- ✗   Well I'm going to get back to some questions about KISS, and we'll see where we get to. One of the things you've done on stage is your fire-eating. How and why did you start doing that?

- ✗   What about throwing up blood?

- ✗   What was the age of your audience when KISS started to perform? [To this, Simmons responded, "That's a good question."]

- ✗   Do you have any memories of life in Israel?

- ✗   Were you from an orthodox family?

- ✗   What's your mother's reaction to KISS?

The shift in questioning style to focus on discovery was like an oar turning a boat.

There was no such turning point in Lauren Green's July 20, 2013 interview with Dr. Reza Aslan on Fox News—one of the most prejudicial interviews I have ever heard. Aslan is a religious scholar and historian who was ostensibly being interviewed about his new book, *Zealot: The Life and Times of Jesus of Nazareth*. Of note is that Aslan has four advanced degrees in his field, including one in the New Testament, and he included roughly 100 pages of endnotes to provide full disclosure on his source material for the book.

Green's questions themselves were often hotly delivered and interspersed with criticism of the book from other people—suggesting that Green had not read the book herself—and would leave many people wondering about the true intent of the nine-minute interview:

- ✗ You're a Muslim, so why did you write a book about the founder of Christianity?

- ✗ Why would you be interested in the founder of Christianity?

- ✗ How are your findings different from what Islam actually believes about Jesus?

- ✗ [After noting a criticism of one person who said that some of Aslan's claims had "been abandoned and refuted," Green posed the question,] What do you say to that?

- ✗ What are your conclusions about Jesus?

- ✗ [After reading a Twitter comment from someone who criticized the bias of the book and said, "That's like a having a Democrat writing a book about why Reagan wasn't a good Republican," Green asked,] What do you say to that?

- ✗ Why would a Democrat want to promote democracy by writing about a Republican?[8]

The structure of the questions is actually fine, and, in reading them without hearing them or the responses, you might easily conclude that the furor over the interview was inflated. Questioning bias does not necessarily emerge from the question alone, however. The style of delivery can change everything. Asking, "Who are you?" can signal anger, fear, amazement, humor, or sarcasm, as well as simple curiosity about a person's identity.

In asking questions, remember what your mother probably told you at least once a week, especially when you were a teenager: "Watch your tone of voice!" You can ask a question that's been scripted for you by a lawyer for job interviews and still be justifiably accused of bias or other inappropriateness. For example, if you're a man asking a beautiful female applicant, "How did you get along with your last boss?" you could find yourself in trouble if the inflection on "get along" suggests that you're asking about more than a work relationship.

SIZE MATTERS

Another element of structure is the size of a question. To illustrate this idea, put your arms straight out in front of you, with your palms facing each other. Visualize a question fitting into that space. That's the size of a good question. Now extend your arms to create an obtuse angle of about 160 degrees. Visualize a question fitting into that space. That's the size of a question that's probably bad.

What kind of bug is that?

What do you think that is. . .a biting bug or the kind that tastes good?

Short, simple questions tend to yield the clearest answers. The way to keep them short and simple is to follow the next rule: Ask about only one thing at a time.

Listen to interview shows with length in mind; you will be amazed at how journalists/interviewers sometimes take forever to set up a question. They want to slip in their point of view, to set the stage, to insert a few "relevant" bits of background information. Here is a question posed to the author of a human behavior book on a radio show about a State of the Union address by President Barack Obama: "Given that the colors red and blue are associated with the different parties, what are your insights on the fact that not only did the President wear a purple tie, but also Speaker of the House John Boehner—knowing as we do, of course, that purple is a combination of blue and red?" Even though the interviewer used an interrogative, the question was so stuffed with details that the end result was a bad question.

If you have a good question, you don't have to do a lot of setup. Ask a good question and it will be understood that you understand the subject. You don't have to embed expertise in qualifying phrases and ancillary remarks. With that guidance in mind, the interviewer could have phrased the question in a way that allowed the guest to express her expertise, rather than essentially throw an answer into the question: "What are your insights on the fact that both President Obama and House Speaker Boehner wore purple ties?"

USING FRAMES

In structuring a question, the best first step is the interrogative, but it may not be enough to get you started down a productive questioning path. Each question has single subject; sometimes it's a complicated or emotionally taxing subject, though, so the question needs to be framed. Here's an example.

Ann, an 80-year-old woman, walked slowly into the office of Matthew, a lawyer roughly her grandson's age. Matthew could tell she seemed reticent, and, after offering her a comfortable chair and a cup of coffee, he sat down in a chair facing hers; there was no desk or table between them. "I'll need to ask you a lot of questions, Ann," he began. She said she understood. Instead of launching into a series of questions, however, Matthew wisely opened with, "Estate planning means different things to different people, so we need to focus first on who is important to *you*." He waited a couple of seconds so she could digest that, and then he asked, "Who comes to mind for you when you think about estate planning?"

After Ann responded by talking about her two children, their spouses, and her two grandchildren, Matthew commented, "It sounds as though you have a loving, happy family, Ann. How do you think our work together will help them?"

Matthew used a technique I call *framing* throughout his questioning of Ann. This is a way of supplying information or comments that help the person answer your questions. Physicians do it when they open with, "I want to talk to you about your medical history," as opposed to something akin to "What's wrong with you today?" The framer sets the tone in addition to introducing the subject of the upcoming question.

Keep this technique in mind as you proceed through the next chapter and consider leading questions. Leading questions are bad questions that many people use instead of relying on framers. The difference is that framing a question does not suggest an answer to the question, whereas leading questions do.

Chapter 3
Question Types

Questioning is a straight beam of light; we're putting it through a prism so you can see all facets of it and the different results that can come out of the process.

There are categories of good questions and bad questions. In the world of interrogation, so-called bad questions are sometimes useful, and I will explain why in this chapter. The emphasis here is on asking good questions, but depending on your reasons for reading this book, you may have cause to employ bad questions to confuse someone deliberately or to destabilize him or her in a kind of intellectual martial arts move. The aim would be to make your subject more vulnerable to your probing. This could be true for someone in law enforcement, code enforcement, criminal justice, or other environments in which you are dealing with suspects and/or suspect information. And although it sounds like I'm beating up on journalists, the fact is that many of them routinely ask bad questions—and it isn't always because they don't know the difference. They do it intentionally to catch candidates and celebrities off guard.

GOOD QUESTIONS

There are six types of good questions: direct, control, repeat, persistent, summary, and non-pertinent. To describe them briefly:

1. **Direct**—You pose a simple question with a basic interrogative.

2. **Control**—You already know the answer to it when you ask it. It's a way of finding out whether or not the person is lying, uninformed, and/or not paying attention.

3. **Repeat**—You ask two different questions that are after the same information.

4. **Persistent**—You ask the same question in different ways to explore all facets of the desired information.

5. **Summary**—You ask a question that is intended to allow the source an opportunity to revisit the answer.

6. **Non-pertinent**—It doesn't pertain to the subject you really want to know about, but it's one the person will probably not lie about; it serves the purpose of seeing what the truth "looks like" and getting the person to open up to you. It can also tie in to the context of the questioning exchange.

Direct

Think back to the Santa Claus exercise I did with Judith as part of Chapter 1. All of those simple questions she asked were direct. Direct questions are the best: One interrogative, one verb, and one noun or pronoun.

✗ Who are you?

✗ What happened at the party?

✗ When did you arrive at the office?

✗ Where are the car keys?

✗ Why did you leave the meeting early?

✗ How much did you pay for that iPad?

Eric Maddox, the Army Staff Sergeant who was awarded the Legion of Merit, the Bronze Star, and other distinctions for his prominent role in capturing Saddam Hussein, was one of the interrogators we trained at Ft. Huachuca. In his book, *Mission: Black List #1*, he recounts a critical interrogation of a fisherman whose information led him directly to Saddam's #2. Maddox's time in Tikrit was nearing the end, and being pressed for time, he simply asked a series of direct questions—embedding a sort of coercive rapport-building into the exchange:

"How long have you lived in Samarra?" I asked.

"My whole life."

"How long have you owned the fish farm?"

"For only a month."

"How did you get it?"

"It was given to me by my mother's family."

"Who gave it to you?"

"My mother's brother. My uncle. He is dead."

I glared at him. "If he's dead, how could he give you the fish farm?"

"It was his son," he stammered. "My cousin. He is dead, too."

I almost laughed. Did this guy hear dead people? "Listen, asshole," I shouted. "I want the name of someone alive. Who gave you the pond?"

He was quaking now. "My cousin," he told me at last. "He has a business partner. He gave me the pond."

"What is your cousin's name? The one who is still alive."

"Muhammad," he said in a voice barely above a whisper.

"Muhammad what?" I demanded.

"Muhammad Khudayr."[1]

With that uncomplicated line of questioning, Maddox got the link he needed to Muhammad Ibrahim, the cousin's business partner and Saddam's #2. This interrogation is a prime example of the quality of information a good questioner can get by staying on track with direct questions.

I would point out two things to keep in mind about this exchange as you proceed to the discussion of the next two good types of questions, control and repeat:

1. Maddox had a great deal of certainty who the cousin named Muhammad was, but he pressed the source for the answer. A truthful answer meant that Maddox could proceed with this line of direct questioning and likely get reliable answers.

2. The "who gave you the fish farm" question was asked three times in slightly different ways.

Control

When do you say, "I'm deliberately not going to ask a direct question"? When you check the truthfulness or accuracy of a response. Then you use a control question and look for consistency.

Control questions are questions you already know the answer to, so they are not about discovery of information. They are about discovery of behavior, patterns of speech, and level of truthfulness or accuracy. Perhaps it's something you talked about before with the person. For example, if you know that someone on your human resources team alienated an employee because the employee sent an e-mail to complain about the HR person, you might ask a control question similar to, "How did it go in the performance review with Pamela today?" You already have the information; you just want to find out how your HR person answers the question.

Not long ago, I asked a direct question that immediately morphed into a control question. The situation required an immediate response to remedy a serious situation. I was introduced to Matt, a U.S. Army soldier home on leave, and I asked the normal questions I would ask any service member in general conversation, such as, "Where are you stationed?" "What is your military specialty [job]?" And in this case, I asked him when his leave would end and he would have to return to his military post. At that moment, he broke eye-contact, looking down. His voice weakened when he said, "I'm not sure."

If there's one thing I learned in my 20 years as a soldier in the U.S. Army, it's that every service member knows exactly when he has to return from leave, down to the minute, because everybody wants to take full advantage of leave time. With my interrogation hat on I asked, "What exactly do you mean, you are not sure?" I knew the answer before I heard it: He was Absent Without Leave (AWOL), and in this case, for more than three months. Personally I don't agree with ever going AWOL, but keeping my personal bias out of the situation—and before he had much time to think about it—I painted a bleak picture of his predicament. The pressure was on for him to do the right thing. From the dark, overhanging dread, I offered a little light and said that even though I didn't like the situation he was in, I believed I could help. That brought an immediate and positive response, and even though he eventually suffered embarrassment, loss of pay, loss of rank, and was eventually released from the Army, I am glad that I was able to help him and his situation before it could have gotten much worse.

All of the actions that ensued resulted from my asking a simple direct question, knowing some control information, observing as well as listening, and staying neutral in my personal response.

A common way to use control questions is to steer the conversation to a subject you know a lot about. Let's say it's Indy car racing, which is something I happen to know about because I've followed the sport for more than 50 years. The person I'm talking with shows great enthusiasm for the topic, "Oh, I love the Indy 500!" So I might ask a few "what do you think of this driver or that design" types of control questions to determine if the person really is an enthusiast or if he's exaggerating his interest for some reason. If his knowledge doesn't match his emotion, I might wonder if other information he's told me about other subjects is a bit off the truth.

I want to draw a distinction between a control question and what I refer to as *controlling questioning*. Controlling questioning utilizes forms of control questions, but the whole flow of the exchange is designed to confirm or deny information that you believe you already have. For example, you are selling subscriptions to a pricey database with deep analysis of corporate performance, senior leadership, and growth prospects. You suspect that the prospect you are discussing the subscription plan with cannot afford it, but desperately wants access to the information to meet some short-term need. You ask, "What needs do you have for the information?"

"We have an ongoing need to provide clients with competitive information for their strategic planning purposes."

What other needs do you have for the information?

"That's it—that's a lot!"

Why do you think this is the best database for you?

"Reputation. I think everyone knows this is the best database around."

What other databases have you considered?

"None, really. We think yours is the best."

That's a great compliment, and, of course, I think we deserve it. How do you think our database would help you serve your clients? [This is a control question. The prospect already stated that clients need the information for strategic planning purposes.]

"It would help them, especially right now, in making some action plans for the next quarter." [You detect an urgency that wasn't there before. Instead of strategic planning, it now appears the prospect is focused on competitive information that primarily serves an immediate, rather than ongoing, need.]

When do you want to start the subscription?

"Right away, so if you could give us a 24-hour free trial, we can make a decision by tomorrow."

> *How familiar are you with how to use the
> database?*

"I know it well. I used to use it where I worked last year."

At this point, red flags go up for you. The company does grant 24-hour trials to prospects who are unfamiliar with the product. In this case, the prospect already knows the database and could spend the next day simply extracting information with no intention of paying for ongoing access. You say to the prospect, "We would be happy to accommodate you, but we will need to keep your credit card information on file and bill you for the subscription at the end of the trial." The prospect says, "Thank you, we'll have to discuss it. I'll get back to you."

Repeat

You want to come at the same information in two different ways. For example, if I asked, "How many soldiers are in XYZ platoon?" the solider I'm speaking with might respond, "There are 22 soldiers in the First Platoon of Alpha Company." Later on, when I'm talking with him about something different—weapons, for example—I might ask, "How many M-16s do you have?" He might respond, "22," which is a way of confirming the number of personnel in the XYZ platoon. It's not an absolute test, but it gives value and credence to what he said before. They are two different questions that cross-check the information provided.

In using repeat questions, you may also uncover discrepancies. If my soldier in this example responds that there are 30 M-16s, I would want some clarification. Maybe there's a perfectly good reason—the platoon normally has a complement of 30, but eight are currently training elsewhere—but the response does give rise to doubt, because there is a mismatch between the number of personnel and the number of weapons. That mismatch must lead to further questioning to resolve the issue.

Here's another example. Deborah was making a pitch for public relations services to a startup technology company. She asked, "When do you expect to have the product ready for launch?" The CEO replied, "Three months." They continued the conversation, focusing on a campaign timeline that centered on the specified launch date. A little while later, she turned to the CEO and asked how many units would be available to demonstrate at the big trade show, which happened to be coming up in exactly three months. "The product won't be out of beta by show time," he said. Deborah's repeat question flagged a problem with the anticipated delivery date.

Persistent

In any exchange in which more than one answer might be given to a question, use persistent questioning to get a complete answer. Similar to repeat questions, persistent questions are useful if you suspect that the person is not being truthful.

"Where did you go on your vacation to California?" might elicit the answer, "Disneyland." Although it's possible that Disneyland is the only place your friend went, it's logical to follow that question with, "Where else?" Bypassing that repeat question and going straight to questions about Disneyland means that you miss the opportunity to get a complete picture of your friend's California trip unless that information happens to leak out at some other time.

Persistent questions also help you check out a person's story. For example, F. Lee Bailey's cross-examination of Sgt. David Rossi of the Los Angeles Police Department during the O.J. Simpson murder trial involves multiple variations of the same questions—a technique he used with such shrewdness that he destroyed Rossi as a witness. Without making any criticism of the structure of Bailey's questions, I want to point out how skillfully he repeated concepts and keywords in a successful effort to make the witness seem illogical. For the most part, I've omitted Rossi's responses—you can easily guess the substance of most of them—to focus on the content of Bailey's questions.

To set the stage, Bailey begins with a statement: "Experience would teach that anytime you walk upon the ground you may affect what is already there." In the minutes that followed, he asked questions that revolved around the notion of whether or not footprints were visible at the crime scene. Bailey's first few questions (captured here nearly in their entirety) included this sequence:

✗   Do you know what a footprint looks like?

✗   Can it be seen with the naked eye?

✗   Don't you know that many footprints can't be seen until they are dusted with powder?

✗   Did you know that some footprints can't be seen until shown with an oblique light?

✗   Have you ever heard that in all of your training at the 300 homicides you've been at?

✗   You also, I believe, told us that your only duty to preserve evidence was only to preserve that which is obvious. Was that your statement?

✗   And if evidence is not obvious to you, it's okay to obliterate it—is that correct? [Rossi denies this.]

✗   Then why did you restrict your obligation to preserve obvious evidence?

✗   What about evidence that's not obvious, like fingerprints on glasses?

✗   And if something significant can't be seen, can you avoid stepping on it?[2]

Bailey kept hammering on the visibility—or non-visibility—of footprints until Sgt. Rossi came across as confused and possibly inept. One lesson we can learn from Bailey's cross-examination is that repeat questions can be artfully constructed by weaving a common thread through multiple different questions. Asking a single, straightforward question such as, "Were there any bloody footprints at the crime scene?" would not have raised as many doubts in the minds of jurors, nor exposed the witness's weak spots. But using a persistent/rephrase approach planted myriad doubts and made the witness seem unreliable.

Summary

Summary questions aren't about determining veracity as much as feeding back to the source what she has said so she has the opportunity to think, "Did I actually say what I meant to say?"

For example, let's say you sell cars of all kinds, from two-door hatchbacks to full-size luxury models. A young couple comes to the showroom and asks to test-drive one of the luxury models.

"What will you use the car for most of the time?" you ask.

"Commuting back and forth to work. We work in the same building," she says.

"What else will you use the car for?"

"Trips on weekends to see my parents. Stuff like that." She pauses and adds, "They live a hundred miles away."

"Why you think the luxury car is the best choice?"

They exchange a glance. He says, "We like it better than the others."

"What's your favorite color?" you ask, looking straight at her.

"Red."

"So let me see if I got this right. I hear you say you want a red, full-size car in the luxury class. How does this description fit what you want?" [You have framed your summary question with pertinent information in this case.]

They exchange another glance. He says, "We think a more subdued color might be better."

"What about the luxury model makes you think it's the best one for you?" [Again, this is a way of summarizing and verifying what you have heard. You want to find out if they are just so enamored with the look of the expensive car that they don't want to consider anything else, or if the first answer was disguising a salient fact.]

"My dad says this is the safest car on the road."

The answer to the summary question tells you they may, in fact, like it, but not because of how it looks. You read between the lines. They are just getting started in their life together. Her dad has probably sent them to the dealership to buy "the safest car on the road," which he will help them buy. You decide to proceed with the sale, knowing that the down payment and loan application will probably give you the rest of the story.

Some people may not be comfortable asking a summary question such as those embedded in this sales encounter because they don't want to look simple-minded or inattentive. If you ask the question exactly the same way you asked it the first time, then that might be a valid conclusion. You also don't want to ask the same question two times in a row even if you do change the phrasing. By putting some distance between the first time you pose the question and the second, and rephrasing the question slightly, you should simply come across as someone who's really interested in what the other person has to say.

Non-Pertinent

You might detect that the person answering your questions seems stressed out; a non-pertinent question could mitigate the tension. Or, maybe you need time to think or refer to your notes, so you use the question just to buy you a little space and time.

In his book, *Business Confidential,* former Central Intelligence Agency operative Peter Earnest discusses the importance to the CIA—and to companies—of doing behavioral interviewing. These would be interviews to probe the candidate's decision-making style, strategic thinking, approach to difficult situations, and so on. Such interviewing is a complement to assessments such as the Myers-Briggs Type Indicator, for example. Behavioral interviewing can be a perfect situation in which to use non-pertinent questions.

In asking pointed questions such as, "What project did you undertake in the past that failed?" and "How did you try to fix the problem?" you can easily make a candidate feel as though he's in the middle of a battle-field interrogation. The candidate might say, "I tried to address the problem by rallying the department around a common goal—the way I get my son's little league team to focus on hitting the ball." You can give the candidate a break by asking, "How long have you coached little league?" before you return to the discussion of his screw-up and how he attempted to fix it.

Before examining bad questions, let's spotlight two ways to ruin questions that start off with all the requisite components and end up falling short of "good."

1. Adding too many qualifiers or other words and phrases that distract from the question. For example, "What did you have for breakfast at the diner where the vinyl counter stools are cracked and covered with duct tape?"

2. Not waiting for an answer is also very common. You ask, "What's your favorite meal?" The person thinks a moment rather than responding immediately. You chime in, "Roast beef?" *Silence* is an effective questioning tool. Don't lose the discovery, the information, and the leads as a result of opening your mouth when you need to open your ears. As the Greek philosopher Epictetus is credited with saying, "We have two ears and one mouth so that we can listen twice as much as we speak."

BAD QUESTIONS

Even "bad" questions can sometimes be useful, depending on the circumstances, but it's important to know the distinctions up front. There are four types of bad questions: leading, negative, vague, and compound. To describe them briefly:

✗ **Leading**—Your question supplies an answer, and possibly prevents a truthful, accurate answer.

✗ **Negative**—Use of a negative word such as *never* or *not* makes it unclear what you are asking.

✗ **Vague**—The information sought is broad or nebulous.

✗ **Compound**—You combine subjects in the same question; you're essentially asking two questions at once.

Leading

Leading questions are bad because they either supply an answer or strongly direct someone's thinking to a particular answer. Interestingly, the same characteristic that makes them bad questions can also make them good in certain contexts.

In most professional and personal exchanges, you ask a question for discovery purposes, and you often want a narrative response. But if you tell the person the answer you are looking for, the question can almost always be answered with a *yes* or *no*, so you are likely to find out very little.

Elizabeth Loftus of the University of Washington published a study in 1975, called "Leading questions and the eyewitness report" in the journal *Cognitive Psychology*. She had taken 490 subjects, and in the course of four experiments, showed them films of complex, fast-moving events, such as car accidents. Loftus wanted to see how the wording of questions asked immediately after an event might influence responses to questions asked later. She found that when the initial question either implied the existence of an object that did exist in the scene or suggested that something didn't exist in the scene, the person's memory of the scene was affected accordingly. Her results indicated how profoundly questions asked immediately after an event can introduce new, although not necessarily correct, information. It then becomes added to the mix of memories people have of the event.

Her work on the types of leading questions investigators ask and the way they influence the respondent is evergreen. It points squarely to the reasons why you want to avoid asking leading questions if your reason for questioning is discovery, as opposed to influence or entrapment.[3] Here are the categories of leading questions as derived from Loftus's work:

Embedded Assumptions

You are chatting with the sales representative at an online electronics store and ask, "How much will price go down on this model next year?" Your question assumes that the price will drop; the subject of the question is how much it will go down.

To avoid a leading question, you could rephrase it as, "What is the likely price of this model next year?' Then again, you might want to lead the sales rep in the direction of a lower price, so a leading question may serve your purposes well—just know that you are using a question for influence and not discovery in this case.

Associated Ideas

You can create leading questions by linking ideas or facts you referenced before to the current question. Those thoughts linger in the mind of the person you are questioning, particularly if you put some emotion into the expression of the thought.

When ABC hired actress and author Jenny McCarthy to co-host the television show *The View*, critics of her anti-vaccination stance were outraged. Michael Specter, author of *Denialism: How Irrational Thinking Hinders Scientific Progress, Harms the Planet, and Threatens Our*

Lives, led the criticism, calling McCarthy a "homicidal maniac."[4] In asking someone what she thinks about Jenny McCarthy's hiring, you would set up a leading question by stating, "The highly respected author of *Denialism* called her a homicidal maniac because of all the deaths related to her campaign against vaccinations! What do you think of ABC hiring her?"

Loftus suggests there is another way to construct a leading question through association. An example would be, "Would you prefer to live in the United States, where dental care is first-rate, or in England?" There's no overt criticism of British dental care, but it is implied.

Cause and Effect

This is one that parent might use on a high-schooler wanting to go to a party on a school night. Mom says, "If you go to the party tonight, how will that impact your math test tomorrow?" Just by asking the question, mom plants the idea in her teenage son's mind that there may be negative consequences to going to the party. A little reinforcement would make the idea sprout in his mind: "Remember what happened the last time you went to a party the night before a big exam."

Agree With Me

These are the kinds of questions I previously criticized in the discussion of curiosity with prejudice. They unequivocally ask for agreement, and are set up to make it easy for the person to say *yes* or *no*, with a *no* leading straight to a confrontational situation. For example, "Do you agree we need to make sure those people keep their jobs?" or "If that were your job on the line, wouldn't you want someone to speak up for you?"

Danglers

When you stick a question at the end of a sentence, that's what I call a dangler. They disguise a statement, or maybe even a command, as a question. Always short, these questioning phrases often have a negative tinge. You might say, "That's a great place to go for a vacation, isn't it?" or "You want to take the lead on that project, don't you?"

Bullying

When your boss says, "You are coming to the staff meeting, aren't you?" that's a bullying question. It would only be slightly more subtle if he asked, "What possible reason could you have for not coming to the staff meeting?"

Leading questions are a staple among lawyers and law enforcement professionals. Political talk-show hosts use it all the time: "Did you feel humiliated about being caught in that lie?" as opposed to "How did you feel about being caught in that lie?" In cases such as those, the use of a leading question tends to be intentional. The person asking the question may feign the intent of discovery, but the real motive is influence or entrapment.

In general, questions asked a witness during direct examination cannot be in a form that suggests an answer to the witness. In fact, courts have mostly barred leading questions on direct examination because they want to hear the witness's testimony, not the lawyer's. I say *mostly* because there are circumstances and jurisdictions in which lawyers are permitted to use leading questions in the direct examination; it has to do with how cooperative (actually, how uncooperative) the witness is. Leading questions are permitted on cross-examination, however, and the rationale is that the cross-examiner needs to probe the witness's reliability and credibility, and one way to do that is to suggest answers.

In interrogation and debrief training there is only one situation in which leading questions are not only acceptable, but also encouraged: getting directions from someone who isn't confident about giving directions. You attempt to make up the difference by following a proven, fundamental map-tracking formula of directives and questions that may involve leading questions to help establish common points of reference. For example, you are in New York City and have only the vaguest idea of where you're going. You are chatting with someone who doesn't give directions well, but knows the city. You might ask, "When you told me to take a left turn at the stop light, did you mean the corner where there's an outdoor café?" That might be followed up with, "When I take that left turn, what would I see up ahead—a park or an office building?"

Negative

In this type of bad questioning you ask a question and then end with a form of "Is that not true?" Any answer here needs a follow-up question for clarification and is a waste of time. It also complicates clarity. This could be an endless game of verbal ping-pong:

"Is that not true?"

"No, it is true."

"Do mean it's true or it's not true?"

If you do a Web search for "negative questions," you will find a great many discussions of how to ask and answer negative questions—and many are aimed primarily at people who speak English as a second language. It seems as though English-speaking people have embraced the negative form of questions so tightly that rules about how to ask and answer this type of bad question are now taught to ESL students. For example, ProProfs.com, a Website providing online quizzes and assessment tools related to various skill areas, indicates that there are three occasions in English when the use of negative questions is appropriate:

1. To show surprise or doubt.

2. In an exclamation.

3. When you expect the listener to agree.[5]

Whereas this advice may reflect prevailing opinions of usage, I think people learning English—and this includes kids in English-speaking countries—should be taught not to use negative questions. To me, teaching the rules of negative questions is like teaching the rules of driving without a seatbelt. You don't need any rules if you don't do it.

Vague

In this type of questioning, you are not clear, concise, and to the point. If it's done deliberately, it can cleverly elicit the truth; otherwise, it just confuses the person and may yield a worthless response. Here's an example: "Given the general politics in Washington today, we all have opinions; what's yours?"

One of the most succinct and interesting explanations of a what a vague question does—and can do—comes from my former colleague in interrogation instruction, Gregory Hartley, who wrote the Foreword for this book. In *How to Spot a Liar*, he explains that certain types of questions serve the purpose of antagonizing or confusing the subject. Among the types are vague questions. He writes, "Vague questions get you vague answers. They are useless if you're trying to get information, but helpful if you want to take someone down a parallel path to disguise your main point: 'When you went to the hotel, did it seem there were a lot of people just hanging out in the lobby?' Fuzzy questions and answers might serve you best as a self-defense mechanism. When someone asks a direct question, ask an open-ended, confusing question in response. He thinks he's getting information, but it's only remotely related to the question: 'How many people were in the lobby? Do you want me to count the people who work there, or the guests, or what?'"[6]

Compound

This is when you ask more than one question at a time. For example, "Did you see the sunset last night and enjoy that new James Bond movie?" Many journalists rely on this questioning form when time with their subject is limited—for example, at a White House press conference or in an interview with a celebrity. That sense of limited time and access might also drive someone to ask a compound question in a text message, such as "WWY & wuz4dina" ("Where were you and what's for dinner?").

Returning to the presidential press conference cited in the Introduction, we can see that one compound question also contained a leading question. The journalist asked, "Are you getting all the intelligence and information you need from the Russians?" and at the same time asked, "And should Americans be worried when they go to big, public events now?" The leading aspect of the second part of the question is linked to the verb *worried*, which carries emotion and sends a listener in a particular direction related to the subject.

EXERCISES

It's important to note that the process of questioning is not always going to be the same, and depends on factors such as context and your personality.

Following are some questioning exercises to help you use the information and skills I've given you in different situations, and also to help shape your own questioning style. These exercises bear no resemblance to the game "20 Questions," which is not something you want to play if your aim is to become a good questioner. In the game, one person thinks of a subject, or object, and everyone else in the room asks questions to try to find out what it is. They are all yes-or-no questions, like, "Is it bigger than a soccer ball?" If no one in the room can guess the object in 20 questions, then the non-questioner wins. A better game, in which the rules do more to encourage the use of interrogatives, is *Who Wants to Be a Millionaire?* Of course, the answers are multiple-choice, so there still is no room for a narrative response.

To Tell the Truth

The best questioning game I can think of is the classic show *To Tell the Truth*, which first aired in 1956 and ran off and on until the early part of the 21st century. In the show, three people would come on stage. Two of them would pretend to be a noteworthy person, and the third actually *was* the noteworthy person. Celebrity panelists would ask all three people questions to determine who the imposters were and who the actual personality was. The moderator began by asking each of the three people, "What is your name?" For this exercise I suggest watching a few excerpts on YouTube and evaluating the quality of the questions; I think you'll find that the well-structured questions are the ones that tended to trap the imposters—then again, there were often surprises. For rounds of good questions and a surprise ending, I recommend the broadcast of February 18, 1963, which features the story of Polish spy Pawel Monat, who defected to the United States in 1958.[7] For the most part, the panelists asked simple questions (paraphrased):

✗ Who is the premiere of Poland?

✗ What's kielbasa?

✗ What is the worth of a zloty in the United States?

✗ What are some of the countries that encircle Poland?

✗ What province of the Soviet Union touches on the Eastern border of Poland?

With this format in mind, the first exercise I recommend is a game of *To Tell the Truth*. You might follow the format Maryann uses for the game in her body language workshops. She opens the section on lie-detection by tapping three volunteers. Without the audience hearing, she tells each of them that they will be asked to name a place where they went on vacation and then answer questions from the audience about the vacation. She tells one of the volunteers that he or she needs to lie about the details of the vacation. This simple model nearly always evokes clean, well-structured questions related to people, places, things, and events in time. For example, "Who went on the trip with you?" and "What did you do when you got there?" The fun, of course, is trying to read the contestants well enough to determine the liar.

What Can You Find Out in Five Floors?

Using only good questions for rapport-building and discovery, find out at least one personal thing about someone in an elevator in the amount of time it takes to travel up or down about five floors.

For example, not long ago I was in an elevator with someone wearing a sling. I blurted out, "What, tennis elbow?" For the next five floors, he told me how he had fallen off a ladder while painting his house. I knew where he lived, what color his house was, and how long his doctor said he'd have to wear the sling.

Maryann did this experiment in New York on a muggy June day. She asked the three other women on the elevator, "What deodorant works in this weather?" They chuckled, and then one made a recommendation because she had tried it and was wearing it; another said nothing worked for her, including that one; and a third said that she'd love to know what worked too. I think knowing what deodorant someone is or is not wearing constitutes "personal knowledge"!

✗ ✗ ✗

In summary, there are more ways to ask a bad question than there are to ask a good one. Keep your questions simple, short, and to the point, and you will most likely avoid the pitfalls of bad questioning and poor information collection and exchange.

Non-Discovery Questions

Non-discovery questions often do not fit the profiles of "good" or "bad" questions as described earlier in this chapter. For the most part, these questions require only monosyllabic answers—mostly *yes* or *no*—and sometimes they require no answer at all. I've sorted non-discovery questions into five categories:

1. Requestions.
2. Pre-questions.
3. Polite questions.
4. Corrective questions.
5. Rhetorical questions.

Requestions

As the name suggests, these are questions that make a request.

✗   Will you marry me?

✗   Do you want to dance?

✗   Will you let me help you?

The person asking the question wants a *yes* in response; that's the nature of a requestion. In cases in which the person is uncertain that a *yes* is forthcoming, the action requested—for example, "marry me"—will be modified with another, less concrete action to make it easier to say *yes*.

✗   Will you consider marrying me?

✗   When the band plays a song you like, will you dance with me?

✗   Will you let me help you if the suitcase is heavy?

Pre-questions

It's not always appropriate to jump into an interrogative. Sometimes as part of rapport-building you want to use what I call a pre-question, which technically may be badly structured, but serves the function of setting you up to use well-structured questions inviting a narrative response. The person gives you a *yes* or *no* to the pre-question, and you follow up accordingly. Here's an example:

> I have a question that I'd like to ask you. Let me see if I understand correctly—you want to leave your job as an accountant and go to art school to study iconography?

The follow-up questions might be:

✗ What is iconography?

✗ How did you get interested in it?

✗ Where do you study it?

✗ When do you hope to graduate?

✗ What jobs are available?

✗ What other jobs are available?

✗ What makes it more appealing than accounting?

A poorly structured pre-question will send the person you're talking with into a state of confusion. Just as a vague question could lead into unknown and undesired territory, so could a bad pre-question. For example, there are multiple ways to understand what's being asked here:

✗ It sounds as though you're serious about pursuing iconography and quitting your accounting job in the next year—right?

The person might say *yes*, meaning, "Yes, I'm serious," or "Yes, I'm pursuing iconography and quitting my job." Or the person might say *no*, meaning, "No, I don't intend to do it in the next year."

Pre-questions that waste everyone's time are this kind:

✗   May I ask you a question?

✗   Do you mind if I ask you a question?

If you are not comfortable with just asking the question, use a set-up such as the "let me see if I understand you correctly" one I suggested, but don't bother with permission questions.

Polite questions

These are questions we use primarily as greetings or ice-breakers. We may not even expect an answer, or at least not a thoughtful answer. In fact, when the person addressed provides a narrative response, it's often a surprise and may even be viewed as an inconvenience.

✗   How are you?

✗   May I help you?

✗   How was the traffic this morning?

✗   Did you find everything okay?

Corrective questions

Many managers, parents, and elementary school teachers use corrective questions with regularity. The only right answer—ever—is *yes* or *no*, depending on how it's phrased:

✗ Can you try to do better than that?

✗ Are you always this lazy?

✗ Can't you do better than that?

✗ Can you please behave?

✗ Can't you act your age?

✗ Are you intent on driving me crazy?

I don't necessarily recommend using corrective questions. However, because this is neither a parenting nor a management book per se, I've only defined it rather than making a judgment about its utility.

Rhetorical questions

These are questions not intended to provoke an answer, but rather a thought. Shakespeare's introspective Hamlet asks a lot of rhetorical questions, aiming them at himself, his mother, and anyone else who will listen. He asks himself, "To be or not be?" He asks his mother, "Have you eyes?" Rhetorical questions are a legitimate and potentially powerful way to focus your listener on a key point. Because they sometimes convey sarcasm, though, as in Hamlet's question to his mother, using them in the heat of an argument is probably not a good idea.

✗ ✗ ✗

Sorting questions in this manner has become habitual for me. To some extent, a shift in thinking about questions will probably happen for you too, as you make conscious efforts to use good discovery questions. You will start to open your mouth with a "Do you" or "Would you," and then stop yourself. If anyone around you notices, just hand them a copy of this book.

Chapter 4
Discovery Areas

When Maryann was taking flying lessons, her instructor told her she would have to keep "a thousand things" in mind every time she flew. From preflight through landing, he then proceeded to introduce her to the facts and steps that would help her fly safely and bring the plane down in one piece. She asked a lot of questions, like a little kid first learning about Santa Claus. *What is that called? How do I slow down? Why am I landing on this runway today?*

It would have been an easier learning process if she'd had the benefit of my training in discovery areas. When you link your questions to the four areas of discovery—people, places, things, and events in time—you mentally organize information in a way that makes it simpler to work with.

Questioning will be more robust in one area than another, and that could change throughout the course of the dialogue. The important thing to know is what featured piece of information you seek in your question.

Here's an overview of the four discovery areas:

1. **People** may look different and have different professions, and may engage with us differently. But whether the person is a convicted felon or the pastor at a church, you'll ask essentially the same questions of each to find out what you need to know. Because people are different, however, you will need to ask some questions differently depending on their personality type.

2. **Places** can also be described in many ways, and have levels of relevance for us. What questions enable you to zero in on the information you need about them?

3. **Things** have characteristics that shape the content of the question. In determining what to ask, consider ways of categorizing the type of information you might find related to things.

4. **Events in time** take place in different places and at different times, with time often being a significant factor on which you need to focus. Events also have different meanings, from celebration to protest. Establish your requirements for knowing about time/event, and then focus on the core issues

that will illuminate the information you need—for example, the reason for the event occurring at that particular time as opposed to another time.

DISCOVERY AREA #1: PEOPLE

There are a couple of ways to approach "people" as a discovery area: (1) categories of questions and (2) categories of people. The types of questions relate to the kind of information you want or need from someone, and the types of people relate to the way people answer questions, and how you may need to alter your questioning style based on those differences.

Categories of Questions

The three categories of questions are:

1. Personal.
2. Professional.
3. Relationship.

Personal

Simple questions such as "What's your name?" and "Where do you live?" fall into the category of personal questions, but most are not nearly that straightforward. "How do you feel about...?" or "What do you think...?" questions are the kind that may relate to another category of discovery, but they also reveal something about the individual's personality and/or point of view. As soon as you leave the realm of the straightforward personal question, pay attention not only to what the answer is, but also to how the question is answered. There is more discussion of that latter issue in the subsection "Categories of People."

Professional

These questions focus on education, experience, skills, and career objectives. A job interview would be the most logical occasion when questions focused on professional discovery would dominate. Given the legalities associated with interviewing, I would agree with the advice Edward T. Reilly, head of American Management Association, offers about the importance of preparing questions in advance and making sure they elicit narrative responses in his book *AMA Business Boot Camp*. A job interview is not a time to wing it with your questioning unless you have a great deal of interviewing experience. Reilly suggests:

Ask about a half-dozen prepared questions that are broad enough that the applicant's responses will trigger additional questions. They would include [invitations and] questions such as these:

✗ Please describe your activities during a typical day at your (present/most recent) job.

✗ What do/did you like most and least about your (present/most recent) job?

✗ Describe a situation in your (present/most recent) job involving _____. How did you handle it?

✗   What are/were some of the duties in your (present/most recent) job that you find/found to be particularly difficult or easy?

✗   How do you generally approach tasks you dislike? Give me a specific example from your (present/most recent) job.

✗   What has prepared you for this job?[1]

Notice that the "how do you approach" question could fit in either the professional or the personal category. In the context of this series, it has more of a professional flavor because there is more of an experience and skills focus than on a general approach to a bad situation.

Keep in mind also that a job interviews can and should be a two-way information exchange, and if you are being interviewed for a job, it behooves you to ask well-phrased questions to gather the information you need to get the job offer.

Relationship

No man (or woman) is an island. By design and default, we all have personal and professional relationships with others that influence and maybe even define us. Finding out about people's relationships with others requires good questioning *and* listening skills to make people comfortable with sharing their information. As a cemetery salesperson many years ago for Forest Lawn Memorial Park in Southern California, the most renowned private cemetery property in the United States, I was often trusted with confidential information about relationships, finances, and personal desires. I could only

be successful in that circumstance if I were a careful cus-
todian of the information and the information-gathering
process.

In sales, as in life in general, two types of personal information are seldom offered up freely: (1) details about
personal finances and (2) intimate information. So in
asking anything relationship-oriented, even when you're
asking someone you've known for a long time, convey
questions with respect and handle the information as if it
were a state secret.

When asking about relationships, it's all too easy to
slip into territory that makes the person uncomfortable,
so be ready to pull out some non-pertinent questions.
You might start off simply with "What's your boyfriend's
name?" but more probing questions like "What do you
like to do together?" may not come across as matter-of-
fact. If you really want to engage in a discovery process
regarding someone's relationships, do what good thera-
pists do, which is say some variation of "I'm listening."

Categories of People

In the course of your exchange with someone, it may
become clear that you are dealing with a certain type of
individual in terms of how he or she responds to questions. So whether or not your questions related to discovery about people, you have, in fact, discovered what
type of person you are talking with. The need for frames,
as well as **control**, **repeat**, **persistent**, **summary**, or **non-
pertinent** questions may arise because of that. Here are
the four types of people, followed by how questioning
might change depending on the type.

1. Integrator.

2. Dictator.

3. Commentator.

4. Evader.

Integrator

An integrator weighs the best way to answer your question. She wants to see how you respond to the answer and then may attempt to clarify her response, or may offer multiple answers in a single response so you know she's considered that there may be several good answers.

Anna, a personal trainer at a gym, was having her first meeting with a potential client, Susan. She opened with, "What are your goals for working out?"

SUSAN: I'd like to lose weight.

ANNA: What other goals do you have, Susan?

SUSAN: Just to lose weight so I look better in my clothes. You don't have to worry about that, but you know, when you get to be my age...

ANNA: What kind of exercise do you enjoy doing?

SUSAN: I like to take long walks, but I know that lifting weight is really important, and I think I might like that too. I'm really open to whatever you suggest.

ANNA: Why do you think you might enjoy lifting weights?

SUSAN: A lot of my friends have gotten great results, and I've never done it before and I tend to like new things, and it would be great to get a little stronger.

In this scenario, the integrator isn't plagued with uncertainty as much as someone who wants to give a considered response. Susan feels the need to balance her answers. The personal trainer wants to design a program that will get Susan motivated to stick with it, though, so she will probably have to use a repeat question or two to determine what needs to go into that regimen. Anna might ask, "When you go on vacation, what kinds of activities do you try to do?" If, once again, she hears "I like to take long walks," then she knows whatever program she designs for Susan ought to include a walking component.

Dictator

Donald Trump comes to mind with this type, and there is nothing pejorative in that assessment. A dictator delivers an answer definitively. The negative aspect of a dictator's response, which may necessitate further questioning, is that he may present a personal opinion as fact. He may also have a decisive quality to his responses that can be off-putting, depending on the circumstances.

The opening of an interview that Fox News's Bill O'Reilly did with Donald Trump on April 1, 2011, in the run-up to the 2012 presidential election captures Trump-as-dictator quite well:

O'REILLY: Why haven't jobs come back as fast as many people thought they should?

TRUMP: Because they're going to China. China is taking our jobs and making our product and we have to do something about it and we have to do something about it quickly. They are decimating our country just as OPEC is decimating our country with their oil prices.

O'REILLY: How can you compete with Chinese labor, which is much, much less than unionized American labor? What are you going to do—make a law that says American companies can't manufacture in China?

TRUMP: By getting China not to manipulate their currency. It's very tough for our companies to compete with Chinese companies just because, very simply, they manipulate their currency. When you manipulate a currency like that—they're professionals at it.[2]

At this point, Bill O'Reilly does what a good questioner should do: He moves into the question more deeply to try to unearth expertise as opposed to—or in addition to—opinion. The questioning continued like this:

O'REILLY: How are you going to do that?

TRUMP: It's very simple, Bill, and now people are starting to use my thing. The one negative thing about saying it—and frankly, if it's good for the country, I don't care—is that now everyone else is starting to say it, and I started it: 25 percent tax on China unless they behave.[3]

Bill O'Reilly was effectively providing his viewers with both information and opinion. In the interview, he asked questions that surfaced "candidate Trump's" point of view in addition to his knowledge about the subject matter.

U.S. presidential debates are a prime opportunity to see "dictators" in action. The debates the public rates as "good" are generally those that include questions illuminating the difference between opinion and fact. Persistent and summary questions can force the candidate into a corner in terms of what he or she thinks and knows.

Commentator

A commentator is thorough, giving complete answers and, in some cases, overly complete in the sense that she gives you more than you asked for. She may, in fact, provide such a multifaceted answer that it could take the questioning in a different direction.

For example, in a lie-detection seminar conducted by Greg Hartley and Maryann at the International Spy Museum in Washington, D.C., Maryann asked a woman a question about how she'd spent her morning specifically so she could get a sense of her sorting style—that is, whether she was most focused on time, event, or sequence. Instead of giving a relatively succinct answer as Maryann had expected, she provided the boring details of getting up, showering, eating breakfast—including what she had for breakfast and where—and so on. The woman was clearly a commentator.

Here's another example: Donna, a change management consultant, quickly discovered that the CEO of a potential client company fit into this category when she asked him, "What kind of struggles are you facing?" He said, "Well, when you're in the outplacement services business, you make money when other companies are struggling. When our client companies hit good times, then they aren't laying people off and our revenues drop. Naturally, we don't want our clients to suffer financially, but we benefit when they do. So we figure we have to find a way to change our business model to reap the rewards of their success and well as their downturns. Here are a couple of ideas we came up with..."

Donna knew that if she weren't careful, the next part of the conversation would go straight down the track of talking about new business ideas. Without cutting him off rudely, she had to go back to the original question and be sure she got a complete answer to it. She also learned immediately that, in conversation with this CEO, it would be useful to frame her question to narrow the scope as much as possible. A beginning that may have curtailed the response might be, "It would help me understand where to begin if I understood your single greatest challenge. What would you pinpoint as the most important problem facing you right now?"

Evader

Someone who tends to sidestep questions may just have an idiosyncratic way of listening and understanding, rather than wanting to avoid answering because she has something to hide. Evasion could also mean the person feels uncomfortable answering questions for some reason.

I have a friend who is sometimes a source of frustration for me. I can ask her a simple question such as "What did you think of that movie?" and she might answer by telling me how the director has a varied style and she enjoys some of his work but thinks most of it stinks. Her mother has always referred to her as a contrarian because her take on the things she reads and hears often runs counter to what seems logical or common. It's no coincidence that she is a creative problem-solver, coming at situations from a different angle than most people. It makes her a valuable member of a project team, but that doesn't lessen the exasperation people sometimes feel when she doesn't answer the question she was asked.

Persistent questioning can work with her. I didn't get a straight answer to "What did you think of that movie?" so I can just ask the question again. A better approach is to use a frame and a repeat question: "So you like some of the director's work and maybe others, not so much. Given a bad list or a good list, where would you put this movie?"

My friend is one type of evader; her brother is another. He is shy, and always has been. When teachers asked him a question in school, he would hesitate, and if he responded, the answer was barely audible. He has a successful career as a programmer and has no problem asking or answering questions via e-mail or text. Cyberspace is his world, and he's comfortable not being an evader there.

In a face-to-face situation, non-pertinent questions can be useful in getting an evader to open up. If he's a baseball fan, you might start with, "What did you think of that game last night, Ken?" After he starts talking, then steer the conversation and questions toward the subject you need information about.

DISCOVERY AREA #2: PLACES

Questions related to places could address directions, location, appearance, layout, or function. Unfortunately, many people are not good at conveying directions, pinpointing a location, or giving usable information about the appearance, layout, or use of a building or piece of land. Getting the information you need about places, therefore, means that your questioning must be disciplined. You will use good questions to guide people in telling you what you need to know.

In Chapter 1, I briefly covered a conversation with Judith, a non-driver, in which I was able to get driving directions to a place I'd never been. Now, let's analyze the questioning methods that make that possible.

✗ Use reference points that are very familiar to the person. Someone who walks to a particular subway regularly can tell you what route she takes, what she sees along the way, and how long it takes her to get the entrance.

✗ If the person does not know cardinal directions, then collect enough descriptions of landmarks, street names, and left-and-right moves to piece together what the directions are in terms of north, south, east, and west. A person riding a subway would be able to say, at the very least, that the train is headed toward a certain stop; from that, you could make a determination of what direction it's going.

✗ Pay attention to how the person remembers locations and then exploit that knowledge by "talking his language." If he talks in terms of landmarks, then ask for more detail using landmarks; if he talks in terms of left, right, and straight, then go with that. If you take a few people at random at Union Station in Washington, D.C. (during tourist season, preferably, to get a mix of locals and visitors) and ask, "How do I get to the White House from here?" you get a great sense of how varied the description of how to get from A to B can become. Some people will point west and say, "Just head that way and you'll run into it in about two miles." Another person will say, "See that Irish pub over there? Get on the next street over to the left of it and keep going a couple of miles." A third person will point and say, "Go west down that street until you hit 15th and then take a left." Still another person would give step-by-step instructions by noting what buildings you would see on the way to the White House: "You're about halfway there when you get to the FBI Building." You may be out of luck, however, if the person you're asking visualizes directions the way Maryann's friend did when she was guiding her to her house: "When you get to the corner where the old mansion used to be, turn right."

That last point suggests how many people give "soft" estimates for distance and direction, and how best to describe what they see and how they travel. Teaching is a challenge in this area because some interrogation students have difficulty with the basics. After teaching for three hours on how to understand, read, and utilize a map—a necessary skill despite the availability of GPS technology—I gave a class the requisite quiz. One of the questions concerned the various colors of the map, specifically, "What does the color blue depict on a map?" With my hand over my heart, which did nothing to save me from an apoplectic fit, I read one of the answers: "The sky." Whenever you think of yourself as deficient in giving directions, think of the soldier who gave that answer.

Some of the questions and techniques you want to use to turn soft estimates into hard information include the following:

✗ When facing the rising (or setting) sun, which direction are you facing?

✗ [Establish a common point of reference] From the McDonald's restaurant on the south of Rolling Road, just across from the Saratoga housing entrance, what route would you take to get to the Peterson Elementary School?

✗ What type of surface are you traveling on?

✗ What is the name of the surface you are traveling on?

✗ What is the speed limit?

✗ How many minutes does it take to get to the school if you are driving the speed limit?

✗ While traveling on that road toward the school, what do you see?

✗ [Establish a new common point of reference] You said you see an intersection. What buildings are on that corner? [You recognize the corner from the reference to a Ford dealership.]

✗ From that intersection with the Ford dealership on the corner, how long does it take you to get to the School?

Many of us have become so accustomed to having a GPS device in the car, and even on our bodies in the form of a smartphone, that we take for granted that we will always be able to find a route to where we want to go. Just in case technology disappoints you—and it will at times—be prepared with your place-related questioning skills.

DISCOVERY AREA #3: THINGS

Before asking questions about a thing, consider the category it falls into:

✗ **Mechanical**—Examples would be a hammer or a bicycle.

✗ **Electronic**—Examples include smartphones and digital watches.

✗ **Structure**—Here, you are talking about a building or other stationary, man-made object.

✗ **Process**—This would be something like a recipe for making stew or fractional distillation.

✗ **Concept**—Capitalism is a thing; so is socialism.

✗ **Expendable**—Toilet paper is a good example.

Many products today combine mechanical, electronic, and expendable aspects, so it is common to get crossover. A car, for example, has mechanical parts, electronic components, and expendable pieces.

Questioning about *things* may very well be the easiest discovery area of all. I have always told my students, "You can find out everything about anything without knowing anything!" Aside from poor grammar, I find this statement to be 100-percent true. It's easier if you don't know anything because your "2-year-old's curiosity" kicks in and away you go.

Now I want to take you into my classroom and allow you to follow the discovery questioning that begins with a completely unknown item that is identified, and, after a round of questioning, will be completely understood as to its name, purpose, process, components, and how those components work. In this exercise I introduce a black box. I know the students have no clue what is in the black box—and you don't either—because just in 2013 it has been awarded a U.S. patent and is unique in its area of development and application. I not-so-modestly introduce myself as a subject matter expert on this particular device and will answer any well-phrased question and follow-up question the students ask.

I present you a picture of the box:

The questioning begins:

What is that?

"An ELS."

What is an ELS?

"An Electronic Language Simulator."

What does an ELS do?

"It is a training support device to assist Human Intelligence Collectors in learning how best to question using an interpreter."

Reflect back on what I labeled the key interrogatives: *who, what, when, where, how,* and *why.* Now is about the time when the seventh interrogative finds its way into the discussion: "Huh?" I consider it a legitimate direct question.

At this point, I remind the students that they do not have to understand it immediately. The exercise is to keep asking unbiased, curiosity-based questions to gain complete knowledge about it quickly. I open the box and show them the front panel.

Other interrogatives come into play:

How does it work?

"This device, coupled with peripherals of microphones and headphones and an interpreter switch box, creates an artificial language between two individuals. That sound pattern requires an interpreter to assist in communication, much like an interpreter skilled in a known foreign language would do."

Here comes "Huh?" again. It's time to question more deeply.

Why do you need an ELS?

"The cost of training Department of Defense intelligence collectors is steep at best and that expense curve multiplies when language-proficient linguists are introduced into the training cycle. The ELS is a cost-saving device that takes a common language, say, English, and electronically converts it into a simulated non-actual language and creates a functional interpreter training environment."

Who uses this device?

"Many are in fact employed by Department of Defense training schools throughout the United States."

What components make up the ELS?

If you are really focused on learning about the "thing," this is a great question. It's analogous to asking a sales pro at the car dealership questions such as, "What kind of engine does it have?" "How many USB ports are in the console?" "Does it have leather seats?"

In the case of the ELS, I would answer, "Headphones and microphones." I always hold up here to see if the students will ask the follow-up as I've taught them.

"What other components make up the ELS?" I hear this and give a mental fist-pump, realizing that they've actually paid attention. I respond by telling them the rest of the components, including a pre-amp, voice processors, mixers, and so on.

Given time and interest, the students can find out every single detail of the ELS—everything required for a successful patent application, and more. They can discover the components, connectivity, cost, applications, and the fact that it was inspired by the *Peanuts* character Charlie Brown. In the *Peanuts* videos, when adults speak, Charlie Brown and his friends hear only *mwhahmwhahm-whah*. They live in a kid's world so nothing that adults say registers with them.

And then, during the course of the questioning, comes the most important question: "Why do you know so much about the ELS?" and I proudly reply, "Because I am the inventor." Anytime someone is an expert in an area you are questioning, don't ever forget to find out why they know so much about whatever the subject is, because you will then find out something more about the person, and it's always about them and not you.

DISCOVERY AREA #4: EVENTS IN TIME

When your questioning focuses on an event, you begin by questioning a photo and end up with a movie. In other words, an event is connected to its past and future, as well as its present. It occurs at a particular time, but it occurs in the context of a series of events: Something related to it preceded and followed it. For example, the assassination of President John F. Kennedy has kept generations asking questions about what happened just before and just after the event in an attempt to understand that moment when bullets hit the presidential motorcade in Dallas, Texas. We know that merely seeing the moment of tragedy is only a sliver of the story. Similarly, the vision of hooded executioners placing the noose around Saddam Hussein's head is a memorable scene, infused with different emotions for different people. And everyone who has that scene in his head thinks of the events that led up to the execution as well as those that followed.

Using the attack on the Twin Towers of the World Trade Center in New York as the event in this section, let's consider the kind of questions that would yield an understanding of the attack and its context. Guiding the questions is the knowledge that much planning, as well as implementation of early stages of the plan, preceded the event. There were people (terrorists) involved, who used things (box cutters, airplanes), with the intent of reaching a place (World Trade Center). The event itself involved people (terrorists, victims, onlookers), things (airplanes, fire), and places (target areas for attack). Two branches of questioning follow the event: The first is related to what actually transpired following the attack, and the second addresses the intended aftermath that never occurred. Both are necessary to understand the event itself.

Questions regarding the event itself—or in this case, two tightly interconnected events— would include *when, where, what, who, how,* and *why:*

✗ *When did the events occur?* On September 11, 2001.

✗ Events are locked in time. *Exactly when did they occur?* At 8:46:40 a.m. and 9:03:11 a.m.

✗ *Where did they occur?* First at the northern façade of the North Tower of the World Trade Center, and second, on the southern façade of the South Tower.

✗ Events are locked in place as well as time. *Exactly where did they occur?* The North Tower, between the 93rd and 99th floors, and the South Tower, between the 77th and 85th floors.

✗ *What was involved in the incidents?* Aircraft.

✗ Events involve specific things. *What aircraft?* Two Boeing 767 jets.

✗ *Who was involved in the events?* Islamists belonging to al-Qaeda.

✗ *Who else was involved?* People in the buildings and people on the streets nearby.

✗ *Who else was involved?* People in the airplanes.

✗ *How were the al-Qaeda members involved?* They flew the planes into the buildings.

✗ *How were the people in the buildings and on the streets involved?* Their lives were either taken or endangered.

✗ *How were the people in the airplanes involved?* They were killed.

✗ *How many people were killed?* The death toll was set at 2,753, excluding the 10 al-Qaeda members aboard the two planes.

✗ *Why did the events occur?* Osama bin Laden had convinced followers in al-Qaeda that each had an individual duty to destroy designated enemies of Muslim countries.

Notice that the questions were asked without bias. The attacks were not referred to as such and the al-Qaeda members were not referred to as terrorists because then the questions would become leading questions. To get a complete picture of the event—the movie version, rather than the freeze-frame version—you would ask the same kinds of simple, unprejudiced *who, what, when, where, why,* and *how* questions about the moments and even years that came before and followed the attacks.

Is it possible to become so dispassionate about one of the most tragic, human-caused events of current generations? That is the job of a good questioner.

There's a shadow box in the hallway at the Strategic Debriefing School at Ft. Huachuca. It displays an American flag along with concrete, glass, and steel from the World Trade Center buildings that were destroyed. We put a plaque on it that holds a statement that I and my co-instructor Mike Fierro wrote for the students at the School: "Why we do what we do." The job of everyone who walks out of that school is to help prevent tragedies like that attack from happening again. Those students would have a place in the questioning related to the Twin Towers attacks because they belong directly to the aftermath.

If you were an investigator assigned to piece to-gether the most complete story possible of the events on September 11, you would need to use a technique that Gregory Hartley calls "forward and backward pass" in *How to Spot a Liar*. Although he looks at the technique with lie-detection in mind, it's also valuable to help an eyewitness remember more details of an event and to cross-check facts about what has already been said about the event.

For most people, memory tends to be linear. The forward and backward pass uses questioning that is not chronologically organized to get people to remember events differently. New details may come out of that style of questioning. Sometimes, the act of jumping around in time surfaces discrepancies as well. These may be lies, or they just may reflect confusion—that is, the person thought for sure he knew what happened, but when he doesn't tell the story in precise, chronological order, his memory of the events may differ.

In questioning a person on the street near the World Trade Center at the moment when the first aircraft im-pacted the building, you might start with, "What did you observe?" Even though the answer might seem extremely comprehensive about the sounds and smoke and screams, she may completely omit observations of what happened on the street around her. It may not be until you jump forward 10 minutes that she remembers that, immedi-ately after impact, two police offers rushed toward the building rather than away from it.

When pressed to remember things out of sequence, our brains tend to work differently. It's possible to recall things we overlooked previously, long after an event, if it's viewed outside a strict chronological context.

In addition to the forward and backward pass, law enforcement and other types of investigators might also use something like the Scientific Content Analysis (SCAN) to examine answers closely. Developed by Avinoam Sapir, formerly with the Mossad, SCAN is a technique for analyzing what people say. It might be used to detect gaps in information or whether someone has given true or false information. In theory, the frequency with which words are used as well as word constructs differ, depending on whether someone is a perpetrator or a victim, for example. Perpetrators and victims would have different ways to describe events in time. Used as an adjunct to other questioning and analysis techniques, your ability to get a complete and correct story should increase with SCAN. (I'll look more closely at Sapir's work in Chapter 6 on analyzing answers.)

Events can run from routine to sacred to once-in-a-lifetime. The emotion associated with the event will, to a great extent, impact whether or not it's remembered. That emotion can affect *how* it is remembered as well (which is another topic explored in Chapter 6).

XXX

You'll probably touch on all discovery areas in the course of questioning, even though you will lead with one area. For example, the ELS questioning covers all four areas, with the preponderance of facts collected associated with "thing" simply because the ELS is a thing. Some information about people will include those students in intelligence work who train on the device and me, the inventor. Some information about place is Department of Defense schools where it's used. The event in time is the awarding of a patent for it in 2013.

Here is how you can create a visual reminder of the fact that your discovery will cover more than one area: Draw a square and divide it into four, equal-sized cubes and write People, Places, Things, and Events in the four squares. Now superimpose a square that is the size of one of the blocks over the center of the larger square. You will see there is a little of each of the areas in the superimposed square.

This illustrates that there will be elements of all the discovery areas. But keep in mind that the square in the middle can move around—all discovery areas will not necessarily be equally addressed when you question. If you are questioning about people more than the other areas, the square shifts to people more prominently, yet there will likely be elements of places, things, and time present also.

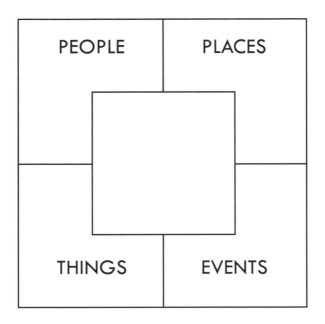

Chapter 5
. . . .
Essential Skills: Listening and Note-Taking

Why ask the question if you don't listen to the answer?

—Maryann Karinch

In 1978, Maryann and her boyfriend began a three-week backpacking trip through Mexico. She had no knowledge of Spanish when they arrived, although the boyfriend was fluent. He tried to teach her a few words and phrases, and then urged her to put them to the test. She went up to someone on a street corner and asked,

"¿Qué hora es?" The man looked at his watch and told her what time it was. Maryann went back to her boyfriend and excitedly asked, "How did I do?"

"I don't know yet," he said. "What time is it?"

"Huh?" She was so excited about asking the question that she didn't listen to the answer.

In a related blunder, I remember a journalist telling me that he was very excited about the opportunity to interview a particular celebrity. He took his digital recorder to the meeting and drew some witty quotes and engaging insights out of the star. When he went back to his hotel room, he realized that the recorder had malfunctioned. There was nothing on it, and he had taken no notes. To compound the problem, his memory was spotty because he was so distracted by being with the celebrity that he didn't really listen to her.

I've already made the case for listening and note-taking in these two stories, but now I want to share some techniques to do them both with excellence. The advantages you are cultivating in your professional and personal life as a result of learning how to question well can be enhanced immediately with these techniques.

LISTENING

If you can't listen well, there's no point in asking a question. So questioning and listening carry the same weight.

One of the most important skills a questioner needs to develop is that of effective listening. If you are not listening, you are going to miss something pertinent. It's just as bad as Maryann asking for the time, getting the answer, and then leaving the answer behind. The follow-up story to that is when she practiced the phrase, "Where is the bathroom?" in Spanish in case she ever needed it. When she did, she went up to a native speaker and posed the question. The person responded and then walked away. Once again, thrilled with mouthing words a Spanish-speaking person actually understood, she never actually listened to the words that told her where the bathroom was. Too many people who ask questions are like that; they are so caught up in posing the question that they don't absorb the information that results.

Another reason why people don't hear the answer is that they are preoccupied with thinking of and asking the next question. You can't be getting ready to ask your next question while someone is answering the current one. You won't know what the next best question is until you have heard the answer to the current question.

Our multi-tasking lifestyle has also damaged our listening skills. We hear a text message come in or the phone ring—these may even be barely audible signals of someone trying to reach us—and we are acutely distracted from whatever we were doing. If we were listening, we are suddenly listening less effectively.

Human beings have two ears and one mouth; the best questioner will use them in that ratio. The questions mean the focus is on the person responding to an inquiry; the exchange is not about the questioner. If the questioner is doing most of the talking, she is not questioning well.

EXERCISE

Listen to any interview program on the radio or television and rank the interviewer on a scale from 1 to 5 on the basis of listening.

On one end of the spectrum—give a 5 to the interviewers—a single question kept Steve Jobs and Bill Gates talking about each other's contributions to technology for about three and a half minutes. It was a rare joint appearance at All Things Digital 5, in which the initial questioner asked, "What has each contributed to the computer and technology? Starting with you Steve for Bill, and vice versa." That's an extreme example, of course, since most people would not have the nerve to interrupt either one of those legendary executives. The point is that the question was short and the listening was long.

Contrast that with questions asked by interviewers who want to expose their knowledge of a subject or person and keep talking, finally posing a yes-or-no question at the end. Those questioners get a 1.

People usually don't listen purposefully; they listen passively. Listening has to be an active engagement because you want to listen to more than what the person is saying. You are listening to *how* they say things so you can pick up on cues that tell you if you need to continue the conversation to seek clarification or ascertain accuracy.

Where does your curiosity drive most of your attention? This is the underlying question leading to tips to sharpen your listening skills:

- ✗ Be face-to-face with the person you are listening to. If you or the other person turn to the side or walks away, you have opened up the possibility for distraction and diminished the ability to listen.

- ✗ Turn your phone off. No, I'm not kidding. If you were having a meeting with an oncologist about the protocols needed to cure your cancer, would you respond to a text message in the middle of her instructions to you? When someone is sharing information with you, treat that person and that information with respect. Treat yourself and your need for that information with respect. If you bother to ask someone a question, then do everything in your power to listen to the answer.

- ✗ Engage your body and mind together. *Active listening* has physical components as well as an intellectual one. The intellectual component involves listening for keywords, as indicated by emphasis on the words and perhaps frequency of use. You also want to listen for the gaps. If you ask someone about her boss and she gives an answer about her work situation that sidesteps any mention of her boss, then you've "heard" a problem. The physical components involve what you do and what you don't do.

- ✗ Eye contact, posture, and gestures can all provide physical evidence that you are listening attentively and with multiple senses. A slight lean toward the person speaking, for example, suggests that you find the person's words interesting. Open, relaxed hands are also more invitational than hands closed in a kind of fist. If you're taking notes, but sure to look at the person speaking as much as possible.

✗   Physical things to avoid include nervous gestures like tapping your foot or clicking a pen. Also, be aware of whether or not someone feels comfortable with your touching him or his possessions. You can completely derail your rapport-building with a person by laying a hand on his shoulder or picking up a book on his table. And watch out for barriers—that is, things that put separation between you and the person you're talking with. If you're trying to build rapport and gain key information from a prospective client, for example, you are at a disadvantage if the two of you are at opposite ends of a long conference table.

So you asked the good question and followed that by listening. Your next step is to ascertain if that's the information you need and want. Maybe it answers the question, but you still don't understand what the other person is telling you. For example, you might ask how a particular app on a mobile device works, but you don't quite understand the answer. That's when clarification questions come into play. Or, you may be skeptical of the answer someone provides you and your quick analysis tells you that the person may be trying to deceive you. (I will address clarification questioning here, and guide you in detecting deception in the following chapter, "Analyzing the Answers.")

One of my friends is technically savvy, although she is not an IT professional. She has the basic skills to create a Website, troubleshoot certain computer problems, and help people around her who find computing technology annoying unless it does exactly what they expect it to do. Part of her service to a volunteer organization is to help them with technology issues. Their chapter is part of an international organization that raises money for women's education and has stipulated that chapters need Websites, e-mail addresses, and other basic electronic connectivity.

When she first showed them the Website she designed, they marveled. "How did you do that?" they asked. This question might sound silly to a lot of people, but there are still people of all ages whose exposure to the phenomenon of the World Wide Web leaves them dazed and confused about how the whole thing works. (Okay, I'm one of them.) The women all knew how to use the site, but they had genuine curiosity about how the site was created. When my friend started talking about the software she used to build the site, she could tell that her "simple" explanation was far too complicated for this audience. She said to her group, "Let's table this conversation until after I think about how to explain what I did."

She came to me and said, "They asked me a straightforward question, and any answer I formulated in my head was incomprehensible to many of them. Help! How do you answer a question like this so they understand it?"

Listening is a critical part of the process. You need to ask the person questions so you understand what they know, what's familiar to them, and what words and concepts drive them toward a greater understanding of the subject. You need to listen for keywords and leads; that's why you want to have someone say more than "yes" or "no" in response to most questions. In short, the process of her answering their question about building the Website had to begin with her own questioning.

What does she need to ask in order to understand what they know, so she can provide an explanation they understand? What answers will give her baseline information on their knowledge?

The challenge: Explain to people with a very limited knowledge of technology how to build a Website.

The approach: Use questioning to determine what they know about technology. Build on the keywords and concepts in the answers to give an answer they understand.

The execution:

IT VOLUNTEER: What do you know about Websites?

RESPONDENT 1: I can buy things.

IT VOLUNTEER: What else?

RESPONDENT 2: I can look up things, like how to make nectar for the hummingbirds.

IT VOLUNTEER: What else?

RESPONDENT 3: I can get the news.

IT VOLUNTEER: What else?

RESPONDENT 4: I can go to Facebook and see what my daughter is up to after school.

IT VOLUNTEER: What else? [No answer.] Okay, then, where else can you buy things, get instructions on making nectar, find out the news, and get a sense of what your daughter is doing?

RESPONDENT 4: Around town. I can go to the store, go the library, grab a newspaper, and go to the high school my daughter attends and ask people where the heck she is!

IT VOLUNTEER: So the Internet is like a town, and a Website is a part of the town. You asked me, "How did I build your Website?" I built it with pieces and parts, analogous to those that make a real place—a store, or a library, or a newsstand, or a high school.

RESPONDENT 1: Why did you even want to build it for us, though? We aren't selling anything, and we don't have any news or information that somebody can't find someplace else.

IT VOLUNTEER: That's a great question! I built it so that people know where you are if they want to contact you to find out what you do, or what you're up to. It's like your clubhouse in the Internet town. People who might want to donate money for your projects would know where to find you. They have your address.

RESPONDENT 2: We're back to square one. How did you build the clubhouse?

IT VOLUNTEER: How do you take pictures?

RESPONDENT 2: I point my phone at something and click, and send it to my son who makes a picture out of it.

RESPONDENT 3: I use my digital camera to take a picture and then upload it to my computer.

IT VOLUNTEER: So the pictures you take are stored in your devices. That means, you can send them to me electronically by e-mail. If you wrote something and wanted to share it with me, how would you do it?

RESPONDENT 1: I'd e-mail it.

IT VOLUNTEER: To build your Website I take photos like that and text like that and use software to put them together so you see the pages that make up your Website.

RESPONDENT 1: What do you mean by software? You mean something like Word or Pages?

IT VOLUNTEER: Yes. Only this software allows me to take the photos and text you have sent me and put it into a template that builds the Website. You give me the pieces and parts and I put them together and build the site. I give that information to somebody who knows a lot more than I do, and she makes our Website part of that Internet town. That's all I know!

For many of you reading this exercise, you might think that this exchange was ridiculous; you have enough experience with technology that basic Website construction is second nature to you. But what if the subject were brain surgery or the construction of the Curiosity Rover on the planet Mars? If you are an expert trying to convey information to someone else, sometimes the most effective tools you have are keen listening and good questioning. Otherwise, no one will know what you're talking about.

NOTE-TAKING

In a professional situation, note-taking is a key adjunct to good questioning. Do not dismiss this skill as unnecessary by saying, "I have a good memory, so I don't need notes," or "I've been taking notes since I was a kid. I already know how to do it."

Taking *usable* notes begins with the four discovery areas: People, Places, Things, and Events in Time. The most disciplined way to do it is how I handle note-taking in a formal interrogation or debriefing. I have one or more sheets of lined notepaper with the headings **P**, **Pl**, **T**, and **E-in-T**. I make all of my "people" notes always and only on my "people" page. I make all my "place" notations always and only on the "place" page, and so on with the other two areas.

P	Pl	T	E-in-T

Because I don't just follow the conversation and information where it leads me, unless there is an urgency to do so, I manage the areas of questioning and will make lead notes accordingly and address anything in the other three areas as I determine the priority. If I am questioning in "people" and a person tells me about a place where maybe the individual and another person met, that becomes a lead note for "place" and "event in time," so I merely turn up the bottom of my "people" page, covering it over my note-taking area, and write on the back of the "people" page the name of the other person mentioned, along with the place, so that when I am logically done with people questions, I flip the bottom of that page to see the note I made on the back, which directs me to the place mentioned, and I then move to places and pick up questioning there.

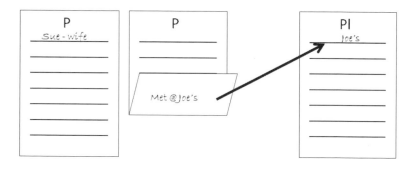

This prevents my losing the lead in linear note-taking. That is, if I took notes chronologically from beginning to end, it would be very easy to lose leads in the text.

Even if you're not in a questioning session per se (you might be in a meeting, for example), this approach to sorting key information is extremely useful. I've seen variations of this note-taking technique in a number of meetings regarding sales, strategic planning, a court case, and so on, so depending on the type of thinker you are, you may already be doing this. I once saw a young man in a meeting sort information on his notepad by drawing a few vertical lines. Each column was an area being discussed in the meeting, and each row was a bit that someone at the meeting had contributed about that subject area. It isn't exactly a people/places/things/events grouping, but it did employ the same essential organizing principle, though he didn't realize he was following this pattern. The salient point is to have a reliable method of note and lead notation; use what you are most comfortable and productive with. If you write small and you want to use a single sheet of paper, drawing a simple table with headers will give you the same kind of subject-focused organization.

P	Pl	T	E-in-T

With all of the tools we have available to us to record information, you may assume that my emphasis on note-taking makes me a dinosaur and this part of my guidance can be ignored. Not so fast. According to William Klemm, a professor or neuroscience at Texas A&M University, in a March 14, 2013 article for *Psychology Today's* Memory Medic column:

> Scientists are discovering that learning cursive is an important tool for cognitive development, particularly in training the brain to learn "functional specialization"; that is, capacity for optimal efficiency. In the case of learning cursive writing, the brain develops functional specialization that integrates sensation, movement control, and thinking. Brain imaging studies reveal that multiple areas of the brain become co-activated during learning of cursive writing of pseudo-letters, as opposed to typing or just visual practice.[1]

Writing notes, therefore, theoretically recruits parts of your brain to make you a sharper questioner, better listener, and keener analyst of what you're hearing.

Just so you can now confirm the dinosaur diagnosis, I'm also going to introduce you to the cognitive advantages of using a manual typewriter. When my young daughters expressed interest in learning how to use a typewriter, I found out that new manual typewriters are still available! When I considered what advantages, if any, using a typewriter rather than a computer might provide, I immediately thought of how it could impact their questioning acumen. Using the computer involves assumptions that you can input letters and the computer will offer corrections on spelling and sentence structure. Using a typewriter involves using your own intellect and skills to make the sentences correct. It engenders clarity of thought and puts aside any assumptions that the computer will "fix" what you do. In fact, I think the sales material for one of the manual typewriters says it best:

> This is the manual typewriter that recalls the thoughtful, well-written correspondence of yesteryear. Devoid of technological crutches such as spell-check and deletion, each of its 44 keys requires a firm, purposeful stroke for a steady click-clacking cadence that encourages the patient, considered sentiment of a wordsmith who thinks before writing.[2]

I wouldn't recommend the manual typewriter for note-taking, of course, but it appears to be a useful tool if you want to turn your notes into a novel.

THE ROLE OF THESE SKILLS IN BUSINESS

Even if people honestly think they've given you all the information you've asked for, in revising a question, you may find out even more. It's very similar to the way Maryann works in helping a coauthor create a book such as this one. She asked me variations of some of the same questions on Day 2 that she had on Day 1, and then returned to the topics and asked about them again later. She also asked me about stories that I knew I'd told her. This book reflects the completeness of the combined responses. I wasn't holding anything back from her, but it's very easy to forget a tiny detail that could enrich the presentation by making it more interesting or specific. Listening and note-taking played a key role in helping her shape follow-up questions for me.

If you do an Internet search for "listening and note-taking," you will find a multitude of university Websites that address the importance of these skills to succeeding in a learning environment. For example, Princeton University tells its students, "You can maximize what you learn in and from lectures by following three easy steps: 1) adopt active listening skills; 2) take clear, effective notes; and 3) review your notes within 24 hours of taking them."[3] There is no "maybe" embedded in that statement; it's a clear statement of probability.

Unfortunately, I don't see the same appreciation for the combined skills of listening and note-taking on Websites oriented more toward professionals. We rely on technology to keep records during meetings and allow people in conferences to interact with others through e-mail and text while supposedly listening to a presentation. These are just two of the common practices in the world of work that undermine effectiveness. I could point to many workplace failures related to poor listening and zero note-taking, but two examples that potentially affect all of us are in the areas of customer service and emergency response.

Most customer-service people don't seem to be trained to listen to a complete answer, and, in fact, they may not even wait to hear the question you called them with. Lack of note-taking—they don't have to take notes because the calls are "recorded for quality assurance purposes"—compounds the problem related to lack of listening.

In his book, *Service Failure: The Real Reasons Employees Struggle with Customer Service and What*

You Can Do About It, Jeff Toister tells a personal story of bad listening. But the salient part of his story for your skill-development as a questioner is *why* his experience is so common:

> Even when we're consciously focused on a particular task, our brain can sometimes override our concentration by jumping to conclusions. I once experienced a classic example of this phenomenon when I called a customer service number to get some help with a password for accessing my online account. I was halfway through my question when the customer service representative interrupted me and said, "That's actually a separate password than the one I'm resetting for you. That one is just for billing."
>
> Great, except that wasn't the question I was about to ask. "I know," I said, "but I was going to ask if I can reset the billing password myself so that I—"
>
> He interrupted again: "But you don't need the billing password to access your online account." Sigh. Still not the question I was trying to ask.
>
> Why do so many knowledgeable customer service representatives find it difficult to listen to their customers without interrupting? This problem is related to how we naturally process information.
>
> The human brain has a unique design feature that allows us to take a small amount of information and compare it to familiar patterns. This capability allows us to make quick sense of large amounts of data without getting bogged down in

details. It's an ability that comes in handy in many ways, such as determining if something is safe or dangerous, recognizing people we know, or even when reading. Here's a simple example. Try reading the following sentence:

> People can easily raed misspelled words as long as all the letters are there and the fisrt and lsat letters are in the correct position.[4]

Toister's story and the explanation for its occurrence centers on our human ability to recognize patterns, which is a blessing and curse when it comes to being a good questioner, listener, and analyst. It is a blessing in that it helps us connect the dots in information we've been told, that guides further questioning. It's a curse in that we may, by default, make sense of what we've been told when the information is full of holes or doesn't make sense. Note-taking helps to sort the organization so gaps and inconsistencies become more obvious.

Having expectations about what comes next or what facts connect with each other are part of the problem with anyone who habitually relies on a script to relate to people on the other end of a telephone. Even 911 operators can be guilty of this script-based mode of interacting with callers, which results in their not listening well, not taking notes, and not asking questions that are directly pertinent to the current emergency. Chapter 8 addresses specifically how this results in a failure to serve the distressed caller.

Robert Baden-Powell, credited with founding the Scout Movements, once said, "If you make listening and observation your occupation, you will gain much more than you can by talk." It's valuable advice for life and work, and I would only add, "and keep good records of what you hear and see."

Chapter 6
Analyzing the Answers

A questioner is an information collector. In the world of intelligence gathering, the complement to a collector is an analyst. That person looks at the information you've collected, dissects it, examines all the pieces and parts, and then links relevant content to other information about the subject. Unless you're a spy reading this book just to find out if I know what I'm talking about, you don't have a staff of intelligence analysts to figure out if the answers you're getting make sense or have deeper relevance than you might think. You have to be your own analyst.

At the same time, you have to be your own body language expert to measure the truthfulness of what you're hearing, to determine whether or not you've made someone uncomfortable, and to know when someone is holding back information.

Here's another way of looking at analysis: When I am listening to the answers to my questions, the responses fall into one of two categories: sellin' or tellin'. If a person is recounting fact and his response is mostly honest and captures a recollection, then he's tellin'. If he is trying to convince me that the information he's telling me is true, then he's sellin'. It is a gut thing sometimes, an audible and visual observation at other times, and it can be a combination of both.

ANALYZING CONTENT

In his book *Business Confidential*, former senior CIA clandestine service officer Peter Earnest delves into the art, science, and necessity of information analysis. He begins by stating that analysis "is guided by key questions, such as "What portion of the information responds directly to the needs stated in the requirements?" "What can we verify as reliable?" and "Does the information reflect both logic and keen intuition?"[1] So think of information analysis as another reason for discovery: It begins with questions just as information collection begins with questions.

Success in almost any profession comes from having what we in the interrogation business call "actionable intelligence"; that is, information that has relevance and practical value to the task at hand. Regardless of whether you are asking questions to find out if you want to date someone or to find out where a bomb is buried, you obviously benefit more from complete information. Making a decision or taking a next step based on partial information is potentially disastrous, as many of us who are divorced will agree. The first round of good questions can immediately yield actionable intelligence, but sometimes they aren't enough; you need a round of follow-up questions targeting the gaps in information. Before exploring the nature of follow-up questions, however, let's look at how to determine whether or not the information you have meets your needs.

Peter Earnest's questions contain the three primary areas where you can begin to focus your analysis:

1. Requirements.

2. Reliability.

3. A combination of gut feeling and logic.

Requirements

Focusing on the four discovery areas—people, places, things, and events in time—will help you get a clean set of requirements, which are guided by your objective. For example, your objective is to get a $25,000 grant for your local museum from a corporate foundation. You meet someone who works for the foundation at a party, but you have heard that employees are very guarded about their giving program. You don't want to ignore this rare social opportunity to interact and meet your requirements so you have the best shot at getting the grant. Put into questions, your main requirements are:

✗   Who are the decision makers?

✗   Where are their favorite places/types of places for giving grants?

✗   What programs/types of programs do they think deserve their grants?

✗   How do they like to be recognized for their contributions?

If you asked the questions outright, you would come across as rude, so you have to be creative in discovering the information. You also need to try to determine to what extent the person you're talking with has the information to fulfill the requirements, so you might start out with, "I understand your executive director is an incredibly bright woman. How closely do you work with her?" Hearing that they work together on a daily basis, you proceed to lasso the facts you're after. In the course of the conversation, ask yourself, *What's missing? To fulfill my requirements, what else do I need to know?*

Questioning isn't the only way you can fulfill your requirements, of course. Steering your conversation toward topics related to them can sometimes unearth the information you want. This is a technique that interrogators call *elicitation*, and it's considered an advanced skill.

Students in elicitation classes I taught had various assignments to gather personal information from total strangers through nothing more than conversation, and absolutely no direct questions. One student was supposed to get a PIN number for a person's bank card. He sat down next to a woman who had just arrived at a local bar to meet friends for happy hour. Talking in her direction, but not actually talking to her, he scratched his head and looked at his brand-new bank card and said, "I never know what to use as a PIN number so I can actually remember it."

"I just use my birthday," she said.

Her friends arrived and they all started talking. A little while later, he commented, "You remind me of my sister. I'll bet you're a Leo."

"Man, you're way off! I'm a Pisces."

"Early April."

"Nope. Ides of March."

Having done his history homework as a kid—it was a day made famous by the assassination of Julius Caesar— my student now knew that her four-digit PIN was 0315.

Reliability

Reliability links to both the quality of the source and the quality of the information. Use of control, repeat, and persistent questions should help you determine a person's relevant knowledge of a subject area, as well as allow you to check for inconsistencies.

Quality of information can be undermined by both inadvertent omissions and a deliberate attempt to hide facts or deceive you. If you suspect inadvertent omissions, follow-up questioning, such as that discussed at the end of this chapter, will help you ferret out additional details. If you suspect a cover-up or deceit, you need more sophisticated techniques to be sure of that.

Deception takes different forms, so to help raise awareness of how it can surface, keep the acronym LIE in mind:

✗   Lies, or blatantly false statements.

✗   Inconsistencies.

✗   Evasions.

Entire books, such as Gregory Hartley's *How to Spot a Liar*, have been written about detecting all three kinds of deception, so my focus here is on how you alter your questioning based on what you believe is misleading or incomplete information. To that end, after looking at a few methods of analyzing content to determine deception, I've included a section on what kinds of follow-up questions you might ask a suspected liar.

A friend of mine, psychologist Dr. Jack Schafer, was my human intelligence collector (HUMINT) co-trainer and was also a behavior analyst for the FBI. He coined the phrase *text bridges* to describe features of a sentence in which a person jumps from one topic to another. They are a handy way of skipping over details, and may be used intentionally or unintentionally, so they don't necessarily signal deception. Put your lie-detection antennae up, though, if they surface in the course of questioning your teenager about where he was until 2 a.m. or while interviewing someone for a job.

Jack's three types of text bridges are:

1.   Subordinating words.

2.   Adverbial conjunctives.

3.   Transition words.[2]

Subordinating words include *after*, *although*, *as if*, *as long as*, *because*, *before*, *even though*, *if*, *in order*, *that*, *since*, *so*, *than*, *through*, *unless*, *until*, *when*, *where*, *wherever*, and *while*. For example, "I didn't know the client was upset even though her visit that afternoon was unexpected."

Adverbial conjunctives link ideas in sequences that are essentially disconnected. Some of them are *accordingly*, *however*, *besides*, *nevertheless*, *consequently*, *otherwise*, *again*, *indeed*, *also*, *moreover*, *finally*, *therefore*, *furthermore*, *then*, and *thus*. They are a great tool for omitting salient facts. For example, during the 9-1-1 call that Anthony Mitchell and his mother made after the discovery of his girlfriend's body, one of the dispatchers asked Anthony, "Where were you when she was walking on the trail?" He replied: "Me and her just walked up to McKnight Market to see if it was open, then she said she was going to stay at a friend's house and she would call or text me when she got there." The two of them "just" walked up to the market and, if this story should be taken literally, "then" the very next thing that happened was the girl's announcement that she was going to stay at a friend's house. Anthony Mitchell was later accused of murdering 16-year-old Anna Hurd on a trail in a Minneapolis, Minnesota park.

"Transitional words connect themes and ideas or establish relationships," according to Jack, and they fall into the categories of time, contrast, result, and addition.

✗ Time: *after*, *afterward*, *before*, *during*, *earlier*, *eventually*, *finally*, *first*, *later*, *meanwhile*, *since*, *then*, and *until*.

✗ Contrast: *however, in contrast, indeed, instead, nevertheless, on the contrary, on the other hand,* and *yet.*

✗ Result: *because, consequently, as a result, on account of, so, then, therefore,* and *thus.*

✗ Addition: *also, and, besides, for example, furthermore, in addition, moreover,* and *too.*

A reckless driver is using a type of transition in telling a police officer: "Of course I saw the crosswalk. In addition, before I drove through it, I looked at the sidewalk to make sure no one was about to cross the street. Suddenly, this woman started banging on the hood of my car with her purse." The cover-up is that the driver went through the crosswalk without coming to a complete stop first and didn't see the woman approaching the crosswalk from the other side of the street.

In addition to learning about text bridges from Jack Schafer, I also had the benefit of learning lie-detection techniques from Avinoam Shapir, who had served with Mossad prior to his work with U.S. interrogation trainees and U.S. law enforcement. His technique is called **SCAN** (Scientific Content Analysis), but a more generic name is *statement analysis.* It's marketed primarily as a science-based way for criminal investigators to determine whether or not a subject is telling the truth, hiding information, and involved in the crime. A key premise is that people who've committed a crime may make statements that are literally true about the circumstances related to it; they just give you the information in such a way that it doesn't suggest their guilt. For example, "I saw the diamonds in the showcase, locked it, left the store, and armed the alarm" leaves out the fact that the person put the diamonds in his duffle bag before he locked the showcase and left the store. There are many more levels of sophistication in Avinoam's approach, so I want to make it clear I'm only scratching the surface with this description.

In the context of professional questioning, SCAN is mostly applicable if you're in some aspect of law enforcement. If you were to talk to a particular victim of a crime as well as the accused, you might actually be able to calculate the time and focus of information prior to, during, and after the crime/incident. You could then compare statements and thereby see what the perpetrator emphasizes or minimizes based on actual word count. The victim will spend less time talking about the time and events leading up to and after the crime and expand on the incident so much that the time and word count are again comparable.

Zeroing in on a person's natural sorting style can also help you detect deception. Some people have a tendency to be time-oriented, whereas others focus on sequence of occurrences, or events. A time-based person has a greater awareness of when he does things, how long it takes to do something, and so on, than do the other two types. The person who thinks in terms of sequence will answer a question like, "What did you this morning?" with a string of actions that probably begins with, "I got up." Ask the same question of an event person, and you'll get highlights such as "I attended a staff meeting, and I had a great conversation with my new client."

If a person has a distinct sorting style, it would raise suspicions if he deviates from his pattern. For example,

Jack leaves home at 7:30 every day and gets to his office between 8:45 and 9:00, depending on weather and traffic. He always allows 15 minutes extra to get to an appointment, so he generally arrives early and waits for the meeting to begin. If you ask him what he did that day, he'd start off by giving you the time he did it: "I got up at 6…" One day, Jack comes home at 8 p.m. and his wife asks, "Where have you been? You said you were leaving the office at 5:30 today!"

"After I left the office, I realized I forgot the power cord for my notebook, so I went back upstairs. Then I ran into the project team for the Smith account and they said they were having trouble making the numbers work, so I went into the conference room to help. I'm really sorry, dear. I should have called."

If Jack's wife knows anything about sorting styles and text bridges, she will whip out some interrogatives and ask questions such as, "How long were you with the project team?"

Logic and Gut Feeling

René Descartes, the French philosopher famous for saying "I think therefore I am," also said, "We have now indicated the two operations of our understanding, intuition and deduction, on which alone we have said we must rely in the acquisition of knowledge." When it comes to analysis, therefore, you need both. Some people might assert that they just don't have any intuition, but I would disagree. It's not that we all don't have it; it's that we often ignore it.

In psychological terms, intuition refers to the ability to acquire knowledge without the use of reason or without drawing a conclusion based on evidence. Unless you're a human behavior and/or body language expert, you use intuition regularly to decide whether or not you can trust the stranger next to you in a store, for example. You just know it.

When it comes to information analysis, "using your head" means both evaluating what you've been told based on the pieces fitting together in a logical way, and deciding, once you've connected them, if they feel as though they belong together.

Bobby was an inveterate liar, but Nicole didn't know that for months. They got engaged quickly, met with a real estate agent to discuss a home loan that leveraged his military benefits, and moved clothes and a dog into her apartment. Normally, he was a talker—full of details about his academic and social life at The Citadel, his adventures in the Marine Corps, and his enjoyment of high-adrenaline sports. But whenever Nicole asked about work, he'd say, "We test things for the government, mostly the military. We test everything from pencils to parachutes."

She felt he was hiding something, but she was madly in love and brushed her concerns aside. Reasoning her way toward a good excuse for his vagueness about his work, she concluded he didn't like it very much. She figured that he talked about skiing, skydiving, and riding his motorcycle because these things were just more interesting to him.

Two months into their intense relationship, Bobby said he had to go on an extended field trip to Nevada.

His team would be testing some equipment related to nuclear waste containment, and he really wouldn't have the ability to communicate much.

"What kind of equipment?" she asked.

"The focus in really on the mechanical stuff at this facility," he responded. And then he described the facility in great detail. He talked about the challenges associated with nuclear waste containment. He never answered the question.

"Yeah, but what kind of equipment are you testing," she asked again. He went into even greater detail about the location, the weather in the area, and everything except what equipment his team would be testing.

Nearly a month later, he came back home. He was sore and tired and he seemed a bit distant. It was the sense of distance that woke up her intuition.

She noticed that muscle pain, fatigue, and headaches seemed to plague him. Nicole gave in to both logic and intuition and started asking questions. Why was he so sick? What had they been testing in Nevada?

As he was drifting off to sleep, he muttered something about malaria. "Malaria? I didn't know that malaria was something people got in Nevada," she said sharply.

"I was in Kenya."

After that, she questioned him until she got the truth. Much of what he had told her about himself in the past few months was true—the parts with the abundant detail—but much of what he had told her was a cover-up—the parts with the sketchy descriptions. Bobby was working for a U.S. intelligence agency and was not at liberty to disclose what he did. During his absence, he had also come to the conclusion that their relationship was moving too fast.

Nicole didn't have any formal training in questioning or lie detection. But she did sense that the discrepancy between how he seemed to enjoy describing parts of his life in great detail and how he talked about his work was a sign of lying. She also believed that the distance she felt between them was not a result of his illness.

Incongruity in narrative style is a red flag no matter what the topic. Someone who relishes going on and on about various subjects, and then clams up with others, is someone you can suspect of withholding pertinent facts. In a personal situation, the spouse who provides great detail about meetings at work and the horrendous drive home in the rain, but leaves out details about the "social hour" that occurred before the drive home might be hiding something. Give in to both your logic and intuition when something like this occurs. When you ask in a straightforward manner, "What happened at the social hour?" and the answer is uninformative, maybe you want to start a round of timeline questioning and highlight "who."

ANALYZING MANNER OF EXPRESSION

Questioning does not stand alone as a way of getting information and determining whether or not it's truthful. Body language and vocal cues need to be counted in the mix of indicators about whether or not you are building rapport, getting complete information, and getting truthful information. Information collection is not only a matter of what people say, but also how they say it and what they are doing when they say it.

You are looking for deviations from the person's pattern, and not a specific syllable like "um" or a specific movement like wandering eyes. Some people insert "um" nearly as much as they do regular words when they are trying to answer a question. You are listening and looking for vocal and physical expressions that are different from those the person generally uses.

Vocal Cues

Vocal elements are how the content is delivered. A famous example of vocal cues suggesting there is more to the story than the words would suggest is President Bill Clinton's denial of an intimate relationship with Monica Lewinsky. The words were separate and deliberate, and he seemed to be beating listeners with his tone of voice—all vocal features that were uncharacteristic of an affable man who was well-regarded for his ability to give a speech and make the experience feel personal. When he said, "I did not have sexual relations with that woman," his words of denial were spaced far apart, and millions of people who are not schooled in interrogation wondered, "What's up with this?"

Here's an example of good questioning. I called customer service for an online retailer and complained that I'd never gotten a $30 item I had ordered. The representative did a good job with interrogatives, starting with, "Who are you?" "What is your order number?" and "When did you place the order?" I answered all the questions—not once, but at least three times—and the representative kindly informed me that the shipment must have been lost in transit so he would replace it at no charge. In addition, the company would do an overnight shipment as a precaution against losing the package in transit again. I found out the next day that the first package had actually arrived but it had been put somewhere I never would have looked for it. I called the company back and explained what happened and we sorted it out.

Customer service people such as the one I dealt with are accustomed to people trying to get something for nothing. They do persistent questioning and repeat questioning as a matter of policy. They also record the calls "for quality assurance purposes," which no doubt includes a record in case there is a suspicion of fraud. Anyone listening to my call would have heard someone who was truthful and merely interested in rectifying a situation. In contrast, a person who had received the item and was calling to get a duplicate for free would most likely have evinced vocal cues of deception. They could have included one or all of the following:

✗ Enunciation of key words may change the third time the person is providing the information, as if the lie is getting too hard to repeat.

✗ Pace of speech might change, either getting quicker ("I've gone through this before; let's just wrap it up") or slower ("What is the point of going over this again?").

✗ Stridency, or tightness, in the voice because stress is present.

✗ Insertion of filler words like "well" or "uh," as a subliminal way of avoiding the repetition of a lie, or maybe because the person just forgot what he said the first time.

✗   Shift in tone of voice, perhaps to a more agitated state.

Keep in mind that any of these changes could occur even if the person is telling the truth. Some people strongly dislike filing a complaint, so the vocal cues are no more than a sign of stress. But the presence of stress is often a sign of lying, so no one could blame a customer service representative for questioning the truthfulness of a caller if he hears these indicators.

Body Language Cues

Drawing from work done by the man who wrote the Foreword for this book, Gregory Hartley, I will give you an abbreviated view of body language cues that indicate stress—a key indicator that a person might be trying to deceive you or withhold information. I'll use the same categories of movement that Greg and Maryann have used in their last seven books, including *How to Spot a Liar*. They list four major types—illustrators, regulators, barriers, and adaptors—and define them briefly as follows:

1. **Illustrators** are movements that punctuate a statement.

2. **Barriers** separate one person from another.

3. **Adaptors** are nervous gestures that help someone try to calm down.

4. **Regulators** are used to control someone else's speech.

Deviation from what's customary for a person in each type is a body language cue that the person is under stress.

Adolf Hitler often used an *illustrator* that Greg labels "batoning," which describes the hammering movement the dictator made to drive home a point. That was a customary illustrator for Hitler. In contrast, when a man (or woman) known for more conciliatory or gentle gestures suddenly uses batoning to punctuate denial of an affair, for example, that means it's time to whip out the interrogatives and quiz him. Batoning in this instance is an example of what Greg calls a deviation from *baseline*; that is, how a person typically speaks or acts in a relatively low-stress situation.

Another way to determine deviation is by the intensity of the movement. A person might use illustrators quite a bit, with arms moving all around while telling story, but maybe those arms tend to move in the mid-section of the body. Suddenly, in the midst of answering a question about why she changed jobs, the arms come to a rest at the side of her body. Or she may start flailing above her shoulders. Either variation suggests that stress is present; the question wasn't an easy one to answer and it caused some anxiety.

People create *barriers* with their bodies as well as objects. After asking a question that the other person perceives as difficult—for whatever reason—he may turn to the side, take a step back, or maybe put his glass of wine between the two of you. Any movement like this suggests a need for more personal space and for separation from you. This isn't necessarily a bad thing, by the way. If you're flirting with someone who does this, it may just mean that she feels nervous at the come-on. If you are in a meeting or job interview, however, it could mean that the question provoked defensiveness. Probe further. Observe any other deviations, and listen for them as well.

Adaptors are those little nervous things we do to soothe ourselves. Some people shake their feet; others rub their fingers together. Some people have really annoying adaptors like clicking ball point pens or tapping their fingers on a tabletop. When you have asked a question and you see an adaptor surface that had not been there before, remember your question and realize that it caused stress.

Regulators reflect a desire to control the conversation. Moms tend to be very good at them, with movements that dictate "Zip the lips!" or "C'mon—tell me what you want faster because something's burning in the oven!" When someone starts posing a question that may not be comfortable for the other person, she may purse her lips, as if to suggest, "Stop talking—now." It's a sign of stress, but unlike the other categories of movement, this is probably more an indication of a question the person doesn't want to answer than it is a sign that anything she's said is suspect.

FOLLOW-UP QUESTIONS

When students return from deployments and we cross paths again, I always ask them, "What did we teach you that made a difference?" One student replied recently, "My source [a common reference for an enemy combatant or detainee] had a cover story with many layers, and since you always told us to continue with the follow-up of the question that gets an answer one time, my consistent 'what else?' led to the admission he was a well-placed leader in the regional network of insurgents." The source later stated that because my student kept asking for more, he thought he must have known more. He said, "I had no choice but to finally tell you the truth."

In interrogation school, we teach a complete block of instruction called approaches, which are techniques to engender cooperation and thus collect information from a more cooperative source. There's an old saying: "You can lead a horse to water, but you cannot make him drink." In terms of approaches, it's always been my endeavor as a former salesperson in intelligence collection to make that statement read, "You can lead a horse to water, but you can't make him drink—but if you make him thirsty, he'll drink on his own!"

One of the many approaches is "we know all," in which the interrogator conducts himself and the interrogation in such a manner that everything discussed is known information and he is simply quizzing the source to determine his or her level of cooperation. It's a game that parents play too, when mom shakes a finger at Johnnie and says, "I watched you at the playground, so don't make up any stories!"

My student's persistent questioning evoked the same result, but with a direct question. In *Mission: Black List #1* about the pursuit of Saddam Hussein, Eric Maddox talks about direct and persistent questioning as a valuable tool, whereas some teammates' attempts to follow up and shake up a source with "we know all" backfired and destroyed rapport with a key source. Basically, unless you have confidence and sufficient supporting information in advance of a "we know all" approach, it can quickly go from "we know all" to "we don't know s#@*!"

In short, don't play games in your follow-up questioning. Be linear; refer to your timeline and focus on gaps of information. Go back to your requirements and determine what you don't have yet. Do you need to ask *who, what, when, where, how,* or *why* questions—or all of them—or maybe just have a conversation and insert "Really?" or "Huh?" Perhaps, if you're feeling skilled, you can pin down the details through elicitation techniques that help to "box" the information you need through conversation.

However you approach the follow-up, use active listening and, when appropriate, note-taking to connect with your source and organize what you hear into the four areas of discovery.

Chapter 7

• •

Questioning in
Professions

Questions work together as a system. As we begin to orchestrate various question types in the pursuit of understanding, we expand our capacity to think and act in smart ways. We gain in our ability to collect and fashion intelligence rooted in reality rather than presumption or wishful thinking. We are protected somewhat from bias, ideology and narrow thinking.

—Jamie McKenzie, *From Now On: The Educational Technology Journal*

Putting together the lessons and other fundamentals of the previous chapters, you can now see models taking shape for how to question well in different contexts. This chapter looks at the structure of questions, types of questions, follow-up questions, and the focus of discovery areas in the context of different professional situations. Much of my focus is on what not to do, because it's the absence of questions or the mangling of questioning that undermines effectiveness in different professional environments. The areas explored are:

✗ Education on all levels, in both academic and professional environments.

✗ Medicine in non-emergency situations.

✗ Medicine in urgent-care situations.

✗ Emergency response.

✗ Legal discovery.

✗ Customer service and sales.

✗ Business negotiation.

EDUCATION

Everything in the discussion of student education is applicable to professional education. The central point is that good questioning potentially helps human beings hone thought processes as well as learn practical skills and facts.

Every year, the mid-August issues of magazine supplements such as *USA Weekend* and *Parade* tackle the topic of "back to school." They look at innovations in education—robots as teachers, mobile computing technology, and new ways to deliver library services—as well as tried-and-true approaches to improving education. The August 11, 2013, issue of *Parade* looked at "7 inspiring ideas to deepen learning, engage students, close achievement gaps, and better prepare our kids for a 21st-century world."[1] As explained in the article, four of the seven ideas would rely heavily on teachers with good questioning skills: emphasize learning, not testing; teach 21st-century skills; "flip" the class work (meaning have students learn more at home and use school as a venue for interactive labs and discussions); and "get creative," which would involve more creatively challenging and problem-solving activities.

Teachers who ask good questions nurture both discovery and analysis. They encourage independent thought and creative problem-solving at the same time they teach the facts. Here is a scenario spotlighting the contrast between a teacher who is completely uninspiring and a teacher making an attempt to strengthen cognitive ability and make the material at least a little more interesting:

Teacher #1 is focused on jamming facts into her students' heads so they can pass standardized tests and graduate. In teaching William Shakespeare's *Hamlet*, she wants answers to when was it written, who is Polonius, and so on. Regarding the end of the play, she might ask:

What causes Hamlet's death? (Spoiler alert: Poison on the tip of a sword.)

Teacher #2 wants to use questions to stir up her students' thought process, and to ask questions of their own. Instead of asking about the cause of Hamlet's death, she asks, *Who* causes Hamlet's death?

A student used to doing the minimum to get the answers right technically, but not thoughtfully, would say, "Laertes." A student who has been groomed to appreciate good questions would automatically think, "Ah, ha! If I say, Laertes, I'll bet the next question is, "Who else?" That student would say, "Laertes and Claudius."

That response logically leads to the teacher's next question: *Why* did both Laertes and Claudius want Hamlet to die?

Here, a narrative response is necessary and a student able to give it indicates familiarity with the plot and the motivations of key characters. The answer could then lead to deeper questions about the people Hamlet trusted, those he mistrusted, and why.

In a presentation that Dr. Dennie Palmer Wolf gave before a group of high school and college educators gathered to discuss improvements in teaching practices she focused on "The Art of Questioning." Wolf trained as a researcher at Harvard Project Zero, an educational research group at the Harvard Graduate School of Education. In her remarks, she asserted the following:

Missing from many classrooms are what might be considered true questions, either requests for new information that belongs uniquely to the person being questioned or initiations of mutual inquiry.

The very way in which teachers ask questions can undermine, rather than build, a shared spirit of investigation. First, teachers tend to monopolize the right to question—rarely do more than procedural questions come from students. Second, the question-driven exchanges that occur in classrooms almost uniformly take place between teachers and students, hardly ever shifting so that questions flow between students....[2]

Whether or not there's a direct connection to Wolf's research and assertions, a number of educators have zeroed in on questions as a key educational tool. For example, Dr. Jamie McKenzie is a consultant on inquiry-based teaching methods and has produced a presentation freely available on the Web *(www.fno.org)* on "dimensions of questioning." He sorts question functions into 10 categories to clarify how students benefit from good questioning. The categories overlap somewhat, but I still find the distinctions useful in exploring the various ways good questioning contributes to genuine learning as opposed to memorization.

His categories are:

1. Understand.
2. Figure out.
3. Decide.
4. Build or invent.
5. Persuade or convince.
6. Challenge or destroy.

7. Acquaint.

8. Dismiss.

9. Wonder.

10. Predict.

To link his discussion to what I've presented in the preceding chapters, think of them as subcategories of "discovery."

Understand

Questions that promote understanding go a step beyond facts; they help make the facts relevant and related. A teacher without a good questioning orientation might give a research assignment related to the coast of California by posing questions such as "How long is the coast? How many people live within 10 miles of the coast? What are the primary types of commercial activity along the coast?"

In contrast, McKenzie suggests questions similar to these as superior to develop understanding: "What are the biggest challenges or threats facing the coast? Rank the 10 biggest from highest to lowest in importance and explain why you rank them that way. What should be done about these challenges?"

Figure Out

Questioning with the aim of helping students solve a puzzle or probe a mystery means asking questions that require thinking, not simply remembering. "What U.S. Presidents were impeached?" is the type of question that allows a student to stop short of exploring the political climate during the impeachment proceedings, the nature of transgressions that can lead to impeachment, and the current relevance of impeachment. Stating that President Bill Clinton was impeached by the U.S. House of Representatives and following with questions like, "Why was he acquitted by the Senate?" would start to put students down a path of investigation. They would be set up to have more curiosity about the controversies surrounding the impeachment.

Decide

This questioning sheds light on options that contribute to the choice of a particular course of action.

In leading a discussion of economic conditions, a professor might ask, "What is the current unemployment rate and how does it compare to the unemployment at this time last year?" Instead, using the answer as a starting point, the professor might pose the question, "How would you have shifted federal spending priorities to improve the numbers?"

Build or Invent

McKenzie notes, "This questioning supports construction or adaption to meet special conditions or requirements."

A lame starting point would be the question, "What's the current situation with greenhouse gas emissions in the United States?" A desirable alternative would be to frame a question that poses a challenge with a scenario:

"Let's say Al Gore has selected your paper as one of the best student analyses of global warming. He has asked that you do a presentation on how to reduce greenhouse gas emissions in your state. What are the key points in your presentation?"

Persuade or Convince

In this vein of questioning, students get some help in identifying prime arguments of a thesis. A question that doesn't quite get the juices flowing would be, "Who are the most successful film directors of the early 21st century?" To engage students in analysis, opinion, and debate, a better series of questions would be, "What two or three film directors of the early 21st century have directed films that are likely to stand the test of time? Why them and not others?"

Challenge or destroy

The question itself directly points to a deficit in a plan or an assertion, and the point is for the student to ponder, "Why is that so?" It's not a leading question because the point is to convey a fact that's critical rather than lead someone to a specific conclusion.

One example that McKenzie uses is this: "Before: What were the events leading up to the beginning of World War II?"

"After: What were the chief weaknesses in the foreign policies of France, Britain, and the United States *vis a vis* Germany and Japan prior to World War II? How could you have improved the policies?"

Acquaint

Questions that acquaint draw a person into layers of information as opposed to a one-dimensional "who" or "what." For example, if a teacher asked, "What catastrophic events happened in New York City on September 11, 2001?" a correct answer could be a bland and factual recounting of airplanes striking the World Trade Center towers. A question to acquaint would be, "How have the catastrophic events of September 11, 2001, in New York City changed the way governments around the world now handle airport security?"

Dismiss

McKenzie's concept of this is probably best described in his own words: "This questioning dispatches that which is unworthy of consideration." One example is, "What is our policy on immigration?" versus a question that provokes argument and dismissal of weak arguments such as "What aspects of our immigration policy aren't working well?"

Wonder

This is the realm of "what if?" These questions trigger healthy speculation and the impulse to explore unusual possibilities. I saw a special recently on the Discovery Channel called "Stephen Hawking and the Theory of Everything," and "wonder questions" had a unifying role in it. The viewer naturally would have questions take shape in her head about the connections of one discovery to another, and curiosity about whether the evidence presented really meant that time travel was possible.

Again, the difference between a question that doesn't engender wonder and one that does is whether it asks for facts alone and repetition of what someone else has said before, or it's an invitation to explore a topic.

Predict

Earlier, I referenced questioning aimed at helping students decide. You might think of "predict" questions that hypothesize about likely outcomes as "decide" questions that look forward. For example, I posed the question, "What is the current unemployment rate and how does it compare to the unemployment rate at this time last year?" as a flat question that doesn't nurture the ability to decide. It doesn't help a student predict anything, either. Instead, the professor might pose the question, "Based on current economic policies of the nation, what do you see happening with the unemployment rate next year at this time?"

The relevance of these questioning approaches to professional situations relates to everything from job interviews to executive coaching to figuring out what kind of grasp a candidate has on industry problems.

Medicine: Non-Emergency

The questioning training that physicians receive for non-emergency and urgent care situations doesn't differ dramatically. In a non-emergency situation, however, the physician generally has the opportunity to use repeat, persistent, and other types of good questions to clarify and verify information.

David Sherer, anesthesiologist and author of *Dr. David Sherer's Hospital Survival Guide* (*drdavidsherer.com*) learned excellent questioning techniques in medical school and uses them on a daily basis. He offers guidance to patients on how to assess the quality of their doctor's interview. When you're more aware of what the physician or physician's assistant needs to know, you're in a good position to make up for poor questioning with good answers.

With any medical condition, the symptoms are visible, invisible, or a combination of the two. Sherer starts with the invisible—a pain. Good *direct questioning* would proceed like this:

✗   Where is your pain?

✗   Where else?

✗   Where else?

When the clinician asking you feels satisfied that you've identified all of the areas where you feel the pain, then it's on to the time and intensity questions.

✗   How long has it been there?

✗   Did it come on suddenly or gradually?

✗   How often do you feel it?

✗   How would you describe the intensity?

✗   Does the intensity differ? If so, how?

✗   What makes it worse?

✗   What makes it better?

Within about a minute, therefore, the clinician has used questioning to address the key analytical points of the patient's problem. Sherer said that prior to medical school and entering a clinical environment, those questions never would have occurred to him: "You don't become a careful questioner until you learn about what the many aspects of a simple subject are."

Patients without medical training don't think the way doctors do; that's why medical professionals call most patients "poor historians." That is, patients only know that something is wrong. They don't tend come into the doctor's office having thought through the various aspects of a headache or rash, for example. They don't think about all the parts of the medical issue(s) they have unless a careful questioner brings them up.

For this reason, Sherer emphasizes the importance of *persistent questions* in a medical interview. Asking the same question again is intended to raise awareness in the patient that there may be more angles to the illness than she's already described.

"Having enough time to ask these questions is critical," Sherer says. "Without it, the whole process falls apart."

Sherer says that clinicians will also use *control questions* in certain instances, particularly when they suspect that the information they're getting isn't reliable. For example, if the patient says yes to everything, the doctor would throw in a control question: Sleeplessness? "Yes." Back pain? "Yes." Extreme thirst? "Yes." Teeth itch? "Yes."

In his specialty, Sherer also uses *non-pertinent questions* regularly as a way of calming people down before surgery and distracting them from the fact that they he is about to administer anesthesia. He asks them questions like, "Where did you go to school?" or "Where do you work?" Generally, they answer the question, and he can tell by paying attention to their body language that they are less tense. He doesn't try to hide what he's doing, either: "Ten percent of the time, the person says to me, 'You're just trying to distract me, aren't you?' I say, 'Yes, I am, because I've found that it makes people more comfortable.' Most people don't like being in a medical situation and would rather talk about something else."

He also relies on *repeat questions*, particularly in trying to ascertain when a patient last ate or drank, which is important information related to the effects of anesthesia. They serve him well, almost on a daily basis, because many patients end up contradicting themselves about when they last ingested anything. At the beginning of an interview that might start at 10 a.m., he'll ask, "When was the last time you had anything to eat or drink?"

"I had a sip of water at around 4 a.m."

Toward the end of the interview, he might say, "You must be thirsty. How many hours has it been since you've had anything to drink?"

"About three hours."

Regarding *leading questions*, Sherer emphasizes that it's important to avoid them in a medical interview: "Objectivity is the name of the game when you're questioning a patient. You have to step outside of your biases and get to the scientific nature of what they're complaining about." Pay attention to this caution because if the clinician is short on time, he might fall victim to leading questions and/or compound questions. Sizing up your situation, he might let a partial diagnosis slip out instead of an objective question: "When you get this pain, do you feel nausea or numbness?"

After the questions are answered, the clinician accesses the database in his head—and probably the computer—to make correlations. He considers, "What problem(s) goes with this description?" The first line of reasoning moves toward the most likely possibilities because "common things occur commonly." In medical school, the imagery to drive that home comes from the question, "If you hear clopping behind you, would you think it's a zebra or a horse?" That's why rare problems in medical parlance are called zebras. When a patient insists that she be checked for a rare illness, clinicians will ask even more questions to ascertain why the patient is convinced of that and what specifics of the problem may have been missed in the initial interview. Again, this is a perfect opportunity for control and repeat questions to determine the consistency and reliability of the information provided by the patient.

Medicine: Urgent Care

Bob Domeier, the Emergency Medical Services (EMS) Director for a hospital in the Greater Detroit Area, describes a somewhat different beginning from the typical non-urgent encounter.

> We start an interaction by trying to diffuse any emotionalism that might be involved. People who have come to see us may have been waiting a

while so they are angry and/or upset. We usually start by apologizing for the wait and introducing ourselves. We want to take advantage of the opportunity to make a good first impression.

We shake hands if possible, and then sit down and try to ask questions that demonstrate both concern and focus on the medical issues at hand.

Domeier has introduced an important body-language element into his questioning and into the training he gives emergency department residents. He notes that research about patient impressions and physician questioning indicates that patients perceive that physicians are spending more time with them if they begin by sitting down and asking questions, rather than standing in front of the patient.

Most of the time, we've already read a triage note or someone else's initial questioning of them. We build on that with an open-ended question that we might frame to indicate that we are somewhat familiar with the person's situation: "I understand you have chest pain. What are you feeling at the moment?" The point is to get the person to start telling his story.

After hearing enough of the story to get a better sense of what the person is experiencing, he asks questions that are tailored to his problem. The flow is similar with accidents or injuries, starting with an open-ended question that invites a story.

Questioning in this situation sometimes involves the skill of curtailing the answer. The patient might start to go down a winding path with this story and tell you about aches and pains that have nothing to do with the primary purpose of the emergency visit. After hearing part of a saga, the doctor might have to jump in and ask, "What is the main reason you are here today?" and then proceed to more specific questions related to that primary problem.

At this point, the interaction largely parallels what Sherer described in a non-emergency clinical setting. Questions like "When did it start?" and "What are you feeling now?" help the physician work through the relevant discovery areas to thoroughly evaluate the problem.

Domeier's hospital emergency department is also equipped with a "blue phone," which gives quick access to a translator in the event the patient and physician don't speak the same language.

As well-trained as EMS doctors are in questioning, it won't move them efficiently to a solution to the problem unless patients follow the path of discovery and don't hide anything related to illegal or dangerous activities. For example, Maryann had a hard landing after a skydive and dislocated her elbow. When the emergency room doctor asked her what happened, she said, "I fell." She quickly realized if she weren't more forthcoming about the circumstances of the fall, that the doctor might order a lot of tests that weren't necessary, so she came clean about the accident.

Emergency Response

Emergency responders such as 911 operators and suicide hotline volunteers need to determine in a short time, perhaps measured in seconds, the nature and gravity of the problem. After that, 911 responders need to provide a well-ordered set of instructions to someone in an emergency situation. Suicide hotline volunteers need to establish a human connection infused with empathy, compassion, and practical assistance. Good questioning is central to delivering both types of services.

In medical situations, unlike the routine circumstances that David Sherer described, there is no time to explore a person's condition from various angles. Direct questions need to be pointed toward finding out what the symptoms are and taking quick action to end them. If someone is bleeding profusely, the 911 responder will often need to jump to instructions on how to stop the bleeding rather than worry about what caused it. (There are exceptions, of course, that have to do with the personal safety of the caller.)

Brett Patterson worked as an EMS dispatcher for 10 years in Clearwater, Florida, and now trains students in medical dispatch protocol for the International Academies of Emergency Dispatch. He has worked to establish a protocol to questioning for 911 dispatchers and calls it "structured interrogation." As he told Lynn Neary on National Public Radio's *Talk of the Nation*:

> You can't see the patient. And you can't see your caller doing the things that you ask them to do...which makes the wording of a protocol or the structure of a protocol so important. And these things happen in the heat of the moment, with a lot of passion. So you can't expect people just to remember what to do in those situations. So we create a structured interrogation that's then followed by an assignment of a resource—what's the

right resource for that given situation—and then structured instructions for anything from CPR or choking to just monitoring the patient, which we do an awful lot of in dispatch until the resource can get there.[3]

Unlike most other professional situations, from routine medical examinations to customer-service calls, emergency medical response is one in which a script is generally a very valuable tool. The old-style questioning instruction we gave to interrogation students was, in fact, a form of structured interrogation. And for the same reasons that Patterson describes—high emotion, sense of urgency—an unseasoned interrogator could benefit from it if thrown into a battlefield situation. It isn't ideal, though. The ideal scenario is always allowing your listening and analysis to shape the next question.

Listening is precisely the tool that makes a difference in many emergency-response calls. The 911 dispatcher who took the call from Amanda Berry, who had been held captive by Ariel Castro for 10 years and escaped to a neighbor's house to make the call, seemed deaf to the information being provided. After Berry clearly identified herself as a kidnap victim and explained why she was calling from a location other than the one in question, the dispatcher moseyed down a condescending, business-as-usual path, asking nonessential questions and repeating: "Okay. The police are on the way. Talk to them when they get there."[4] That message was hollow reassurance to Berry, as she had already been told by the dispatcher, "We're going to send them [the police] as soon as we get a car open."

In contrast, the dispatcher who took the call from neighbor Charles Ramsey at the same time asked questions establishing the type of emergency services needed, such as whether or not the victim needed an ambulance and whether or not the alleged perpetrator of the crime was still in the house.[5] These essential questions were asked in response to what the dispatcher was told; in other words, listening helped a lot.

The journal *Suicide and Life-Threatening Behavior* published a series of articles in 2007 that detailed problems related to suicide hotlines. A fundamental problem centered on questioning—either not asking the right question for the situation or not asking enough questions to ascertain the gravity of the caller's problem. The *Boston Globe* article entitled "Wrong Answer," which summarized the journal's findings, began with a shocking vignette:

> The person manning the suicide hotline should have asked a follow-up question about the gun. Yes, the caller had said he was despondent, and yes, he mentioned he had considered using a gun to end his life. But that's where that line of conversation ended—until the phone receiver exploded with the sound of a gunshot.[6]

The studies documented in the journal were aimed at trying to standardize to a greater extent the practices of respondents, including their questioning techniques. They reflected a shocking finding: In 723 of 1,431 calls, the volunteer at the hotline never even asked whether or not the caller was feeling suicidal.[7] Since the results of those studies were published, a number of organizations have taken steps to improve the questioning practices of helpers. It is not only a matter of knowing what to ask, but also how to ask. LifeLine Network, an alliance of grassroots organizations in 16 countries, gives its volunteers best-practices advice to achieve "active engagement"—that is, "building an alliance with the caller."[8] Questions that can help achieve this include the practical ("Are you suicidal?") and the empathetic ("I am here for you. How can I best support you right now?")

You have to clear your personal biases about why someone would want to commit suicide in order to ask questions that do not imply judgment. Questions like, "Why would you do that?!" would not lessen the pressure or ease the burden of the person contemplating taking his own life. As a corollary, it's not the time to reference religious or social taboos against suicide, or to plunge into a discourse about how illogical suicide is. You have to demonstrate that you want to know what they have to say, that they can trust you with their feelings and thoughts, and that you aren't going anywhere as long as they need you. Your questions must reflect that you see their feelings and thoughts as having value. You aren't there to tell them what to do, but rather to help them perceive that you have genuine interest in them, that you want to connect.

This is a time when the "what else" follow-up questions can be key. For example, "What is going on for you?" may elicit a partial answer. "What else is going on?" may be just the question that will trigger an outpouring of emotions and a more complete story. That might lead to something like, "Who hurt you like that?" and "Who else hurt you?"

Discovery questions play a vital role in keeping people on the line talking with you. Just remember that it's the person who calls who is the one who determines when the conversation is over. (As anyone who trains people to do this will add as a caveat, if the person has already acted on the impulse to commit suicide—for example, has taken a potentially lethal dose of medicine— a 911 intervention is warranted.) As the suicidal person talks, listen for people, places, things, and events, and, if possible, take notes. This has more than the practical value of potentially informing an emergency service provider of location, for example. Having these specifics in front of you enable you to build and strengthen rapport quickly. You want to be able to reference those details so the person has proof you were listening. For example, "You mentioned a Joe Doe, who was supposed to be your friend, but he bullied you on Facebook... What else has he done to hurt you?" Or, "You mentioned that the last time you were happy was in Wilmington, Delaware. What happened in Wilmington that made you happy?" As hard as it may be jot things down in the middle of an intense conversation, having ready access to the basics in the discovery areas—names, times, places, tools, and so on—reinforce to the caller that you are listening with your ears and your heart.

With your questioning, keep in mind that this is not about you. In general, don't minimize the person's pain by suggesting that you've been there so you really understand; in other words, don't answer your questions with your own story. Better to go in the direction of, "I don't understand completely, but I do care completely." Keep the questioning simple and sincere. Avoid all of the bad questions—leading, compound, vague, negative—because they will disrupt rapport rather than reinforce it.

This discussion is important to me particularly because of being a veteran of military service and knowing other veterans who took their lives as a result of suffering the trauma of war. Questioning in relation to suicide prevention is also an area of particular study and interest because of an experience I had a number of years ago with a colleague at Forest Lawn Memorial Park.

Tom was failing miserably as a salesman at Forest Lawn. Unfortunately, this letdown followed his being fired from his job as a flight attendant from the airline he worked for. One day, he said to me, "I'm going to commit suicide." He told me that the reason he wanted me to know was that he trusted me. He followed that by saying that all he wanted me to do was to let him to it. We talked for a while—I had not been formally trained in questioning techniques at this point in my career—and I listened for any clue as to what to do to help him. Finally, he said, "One of these days, you'll get a phone call and I'll just say, 'Tonight's the night.'"

When I returned home from a New Year's Eve Party at 1 a.m., I got that call. I called his number. No answer. I called the police and gave them his address. When they arrived, they saw his door was unlocked and he had taken a great number of pills. He had put labels on his property throughout the apartment that indicated who should receive what.

Three days later, after having his stomach pumped, Tom was the happiest guy to be alive that I'd ever seen. He gave me a copy of Richard Bach's *Illusions: The*

Adventures of a Reluctant Messiah. This experience and the book helped me understand myself and, later, to probe more deeply into the way that my skill and discipline in questioning might help people in Tom's position. In short, they changed my life.

Legal Discovery

In court, attorneys manage information, leading witnesses toward or away from an objective. Unlike *A Few Good Men*, in which the lead defense attorney (Tom Cruise) for two Marines secures damning information from a senior military officer (Jack Nicholson) during the court martial, most attorneys collect the information they consider vital beforehand and endeavor never to ask a question in court that they do not already know the answer to.

Where do attorneys get their information? A primary source is depositions—that is, sworn statements, given orally, supposedly developed through discovery questioning. Discovery questioning should be central to depositions. They are an opportunity to enable both attorneys to quiz their opponent's clients and witnesses, to surface facts and review the merits of a case, and to see how well a witness will hold up in front of a jury. It has proven true at times that information discovered in depositions has led to cases being settled out of court or dropped altogether.

That said, I struggled to find good guidance for attorneys on how to do discovery questioning in the context of a deposition. Instead, I found advice such as "The Top 10 Killer Deposition Questions," which I would like to re-title, "The Top 10 Examples of How to Kill Discovery Questioning." The attorney who wrote the piece gave me reason for optimism with his opening:

> Other than hiring a private investigator to delve into the witness's past, the deposition is the most effective tool in the lawyer's arsenal for uncovering dirt and chipping away at credibility... yet most lawyers don't ask all of the basic, open-ended questions that could help achieve their impeachment goals.[9]

It was a bait and switch. He followed this with 10 questions, only one of which was an open-ended question. The rest were yes-or-no questions, except one, which wasn't a question at all. The list included two compound questions that could have the witness going dizzy trying to figure out whether to answer yes or no. For example, "Did you read any witness statements or depositions, listen to any recorded statements, look at any diagrams or photographs, or did somebody else read you any statements before the deposition?"

To spotlight the use of bad questions in a deposition, I've selected an excerpt from the deposition of Adam James in the trial of former coach Mike Leach versus Texas Tech over alleged mistreatment of James, who was playing for the Red Raiders at the time. As you read this, test yourself: What's wrong with the questions from the attorney?

> ATTORNEY: Alright. And by the shed, I don't think we've actually described it. It's actually more like a garage than a shed, isn't it?

ADAM JAMES: If that's your opinion.

ATTORNEY: Well, I'm asking you. Would you characterize it as a garage with a sliding door and a cement floor, or a shed?

ADAM JAMES: It had a door but not a cement floor.

ATTORNEY: Okay. What's the floor in the room?

ADAM JAMES: Wood with rubber on top of it.

ATTORNEY: Okay. Whose—was it commonly known amongst the football team as the shed or the athletic training storage garage, as Mr. Pincock refers to it?

ADAM JAMES: Well, as players, we don't really—we don't necessarily sit around and talk about the shed all the time.

ATTORNEY: Okay. I'm just wanting to know why you characterize it as a shed in this message to your dad?

ADAM JAMES: Well, that's to me what it is, a shed.

ATTORNEY: Okay. And you told your dad that you were instructed to stand in the shed or else you would be kicked off the team, right?[10]

The attorney asked one good question and multiple leading questions. Discovery had almost nothing to do with this exchange. Questions that require the witness to describe the environment where he was confined would include "Where were you held?" and "What did it look like?"

While I would say that a line of questioning like this fails in terms of discovery, I admit that some attorneys deliberately use ill-structured, badgering questions to raise the emotion of the witness. Discovery is not the point. Their aim is to observe how the witness behaves in a stressful situation.

Customer Service and Sales

In the context of customer service and sales, asking only perfunctory questions gives consumers very little hope that a need will be met or a problem will be resolved. "How can I help you?" is a perfunctory question that should elicit an answer that helps customize the rest of the conversation.

For example, a female friend of mine wanted to buy a pickup truck. She and her husband went to multiple dealerships. At each dealership, the opening question was either, "How can I help you today?" or "What can I show you today?"

"A small pickup truck," was her answer. In six of the seven cases, the salesman turned to her husband and asked some version of, "What kind did you have in mind?"

"We're doing some work on our home," she said, "so I'd like something that allows us to haul things, but also has seats behind the driver so we have a place to put our kids."

Again, six of the seven salesmen turned to her husband and asked a question like, "What do you like to drive?" or "Will you be hauling anything really heavy?"

The banter never got much beyond this with the first six salesmen because they weren't listening—either to the source of the responses or to what she said about her priorities. She bought the truck from the seventh salesman who heard that having a place for kids and groceries was as important as hauling drywall and lumber. He also focused squarely on her, having listened to her words, "*I'd* like something...."

In his book *Service Failure*, Jeff Toister cautions, "Employees should be focused on helping customers achieve their goals rather than following a set of rote procedures."[11] He gives Apple Stores kudos for demonstrating how to use good questioning and good listening to customize the shopping experience:

> The Apple Store provides an excellent example of what can happen when employees focus intently on their customers. Unlike many other retailers where employees concentrate on pushing products, stocking shelves, or ringing up transactions, Apple Store employees are there to create a positive experience for their customers. They conduct product demonstrations, resolve technical problems, and help people get the most out of their MacBook, iPad, or other Apple product.[12]

Employees asking questions that reflect interest in the individual and following up with service that corresponds to the answer has enormous practical value. Apple's 363 stores worldwide collectively generate $18 billion of revenue per year and show an impressive 26-percent profit margin. That means they are responsible for $4.4 billion of retailing operating profit a year.[13] For comparison purposes, Wal-Mart earns a

3.54 percent profit margin[14] and Best Buy is in negative territory.

Business Negotiation

By its nature, a negotiation involves someone who wants the upper hand, but doesn't have it yet, and someone who has the upper hand—or at least thinks he does. If two people who hold equal positions at the table are hammering out the details of an agreement, I might say that they are engaged in compromise or trading points, but not necessarily negotiation.

When you're negotiating, you're trying to get someone to agree with you. Questions can often do that far better than arguments or pitches, because questions engage others in coming to conclusions on their own.

For example, my friend Max wanted to buy a laptop, but every Website he went to was charging more than he thought he should pay. He called the sales department for the company that manufactured the model he really wanted, provided specifications for the model, and asked the representative, "What kind of price can you give me?" The rep quoted him the same price that Max had found online.

Max figured that all the rep had done was to go online and plug in the specs to come up with the price. He had, in fact, simply duplicated what Max had already done. He asked, "What do you need from me to give me a better price?"

A pause followed. The rep was probably quickly calculating how much commission he would lose if he gave Max a better price.

"How much commission will you lose if you cut the price by $100?" Max asked him.

More silence.

"How much commission will you lose if I hang up the phone and buy a laptop from your competitor?"

The rep then offered to take $100 off the price of the laptop if they could put the deal through immediately.

The laptop scenario presents a streamlined version of what happens in complex negotiations. A key aim is to overcome objections. That starts by having clarity on your information requirements, as well as ascertaining the other person's requirements and expectations. The progression of a negotiation from the point of view of the person trying to gain the upper hand could be summarized this way:

> I spark your interest.
>
> You appreciate what I have to offer.
>
> You need what I have to offer.
>
> I win.

We interviewed "Kim" for this book and she provided her story of negotiating a three-year contract to provide public relations services for an international trade group. Her information requirements going into the negotiation were:

- ✗   Who is the decision-maker?
- ✗   Who is doing the work now (or at least some variation of the work)?
- ✗   What's the job?
- ✗   When do they want to start seeing results?
- ✗   Where do they want the work performed?
- ✗   Why would they consider me the best person for the job?
- ✗   How do they measure success?
- ✗   How much is success worth to them?

Figuratively putting herself on the other side of the table, she then mapped out what their requirements probably were:

- ✗   Who is the best person for the job?
- ✗   How much will that person cost?
- ✗   What are the main results we expect that person to accomplish?
- ✗   How soon can we get results?

Kim did her homework on the company by looking at industry analyst reports, articles, and the company's public documents. She also had a conversation with a friend's son, who worked for the organization. He wasn't anywhere close to the decision-maker—this was his first job out of college—but he was astute and a friendly source. Her first major discovery was that "Who is the decision maker?" had a multi-layered answer: The CEO was the decision maker, but he placed enormous trust in his executive assistant, who attended all key meetings. He also had to answer to a board of directors. The answer to "Who is doing the work now?" gave the key to what the unique challenges of the job were. At the moment, public relations activities were initiated solely by the PR contacts at the organization's member companies, so it was a highly decentralized approach. The consultant would have to centralize PR operations. Her contact at the group made it clear they wanted to make a decision immediately, so it was safe to assume results in the near term would be expected. And most likely, there would be a great deal of travel, because the organization had a global presence.

There were also the really tough information requirements: Why Kim and not someone else? How did they measure success? What was success worth to them?

She looked at the composition of the board and realized that at least three people on it would have known her work from other arenas. That gave her an edge. She also had 20 years of experience working with businesses in the same industry.

It struck her that the "C team" had been intact for 10 years, so she figured whatever these senior executives were doing was clearly viewed as "success" by the board. Looking more closely at the organization's culture, she saw an abundance of evidence that the staff—top to bottom—had a policy of "the customer is always right" when it came to meeting members' needs and making them feel special. They did a lot to recognize the accomplishments of members. Kim concluded that a big measure of success, therefore, would be honoring what the members were already contributing to the PR effort. She would be effectively balancing a centralized PR function with continued support of decentralized activities.

Finally, she learned that the CEO was an accountant by training, so she knew the value would have to be measured in dollars and cents. Whereas PR consultants typically try to explain value in terms of "public perception of quality," "increased awareness of market presence," and so on, Kim had a feeling her performance would be judged, at least partially, on new memberships and the willingness of current members to increase fees.

With her requirements met, Kim went to the table and used her information to accomplish a major step toward overcoming objectives and moving people at the meeting toward an appreciation for her value. In the words of Greg Hartley, she was able to "trigger an epiphany." In other words, during the meeting, Kim could hear them move toward a sense of "she's good for us because..." when questions became predictive: "What do you see the program looking like a year from now?" They had mentally made a transition from scrutinizing her to appreciating what she had to offer. When the questions became more time-centered—"When can you have the plan done?" "How long will it take to put the program in place?"—she determined they were moving toward a sense of needing her services. She heard urgency in their voices.

Kim had walked into the meeting having given them a proposal that included a monthly retainer that was double what she thought they would agree to. They agreed to it.

In all of these professional situations, questioning is a two-way street. It is certainly important to ask good questions, but as in the negotiation scenario illustrated, it's just as important to listen for the questions being asked.

What you hear provides valuable clues about rapport, the willingness to divulge information, the reliability of the information, and what you should say next to get the task at hand done—whether it's teaching, treating an illness, responding to an emergency, winning a contract, or closing a sale.

EXERCISE

Keep a journal for two weeks related to questions in your professional life. If you are a Monday-through-Friday worker, there's no need to keep the journal on weekends.

Begin by making notes in three areas of your past questioning:

1. List five questions you asked that made a difference in your work life. Put a short notation as to why you feel each served you well.

2. Add five questions you wish you had never posed. Remind yourself why.

3. Add five questions you believe you should have asked differently.

   ✗ How do you wish you would have stated the questions?

   ✗ How would restating the question have potentially changed the answer you got?

In your journal, keep notes about how the structure, placement, frequency, and other pertinent factors related to your questions has changed.

1. Record one question each day that made a difference in terms of getting something done at work.

2. Record one question you wish you hadn't posed. (If none, then congratulations.)

3. Record one question you think would have gotten a better answer if asked a different way. (If none, then you're probably kidding yourself.)

   ✗ How do you wish you would have stated the questions?

   ✗ How would restating the question have potentially changed the answer you got?

Chapter 8

· ·

Questioning in Your
Personal Life

Judge a man by his questions rather than his answers.

—Voltaire

What can good questioning do to enhance your personal life?

- ✗ Boost your child's cognitive abilities and verbal skills.

- ✗ Help you ease into social situations.

- ✗ Find winners in the dating scene.

✗ Ensure you don't come across as a self-centered jerk at a party.

✗ Convey compassion to someone in pain.

✗ Save you money.

✗ Make life more pleasant in general.

In this list of benefits, some are intuitive and some merit discussion. One that doesn't warrant discussion, but is backed by a short story that makes the point, is "save you money." When my children were in elementary school, our family went back-to-school shopping and my wife and I felt sticker shock at the price of clothes for little girls. I asked the cashier, "When does the half-price sale start?" I was joking. She said, "Thursday. But I guess there's no harm in giving you the deal today."

That was one of my better questions.

Using questions well in your personal life has a great deal to do with spontaneous opportunities to interact with people, such as my experience in the store. If you're walking through a mall and you see someone struggling with packages, that's a perfect occasion for a friendly request: "May I give you a hand with that?" In that context, your asking the question could be the most wonderful thing that happened to that person all day. Questions in our personal life shouldn't be tools of interrogation, but rather tools of connection.

It's important to note also that people don't pose the same question identically, nor do they respond to identical questions in the same manner. Our different personality types make some of us more inclined to question comfortably and well, and others to be less comfortable or adept at asking questions. Similarly, our different personality types give some of us an advantage in evading a question or outright lying, whereas other types find deception very stress-inducing.

A wonderful Website called StoryCorps features great questions in multiple categories to help people get a conversation going. It even includes a "question generator," which enables the user to create a set of customized questions that reflect a particular need, such as conversing with someone who is going through a difficult time in life. The category of "great questions for anyone" features a number of well-structured questions that naturally evoke a narrative response. A few of them are:

✗ What was the happiest moment of your life? The saddest?

✗ Who has been the biggest influence on your life? What lessons did that person teach you?

✗ Who has been the kindest to you in your life?

✗ What are the most important lessons you've learned in life?

✗ What is your earliest memory?

✗ What is your favorite memory of me?

✗ What are the funniest or most embarrassing stories your family tells about you?

✗ If you could hold on to just one memory from your life forever, what would that be?

✗ If this was to be our very last conversation, what words of wisdom would you want to pass on to me?

✗ What are you proudest of in your life?

✗ When in life have you felt most alone?

✗ What are your hopes and dreams for what the future holds for me? For my children?

✗ How has your life been different than what you'd imagined?

✗ How would you like to be remembered?

✗ What does your future hold?[1]

PARENTING AND QUESTIONS

Haven Caylor is a Doctor of Education and the father of 4-year-old twins, Ammon and Carter. In reading some of the material he's put together for a parenting book on traveling with young children (*Travel to Learning and Laughing*), I was struck by the way Haven uses good questioning techniques with his children. The use of interrogatives is consistent, so the children are naturally learning to answer with names, concepts, and sentences rather than just *yes* or *no*. Haven also doesn't use leading questions, so Carter and Ammon are accustomed to having their opinions invited rather than shaped. They contributed this conversation on an upcoming vacation for this book:

HAVEN: Carter, where are we going on our next vacation?

CARTER: Disney World.

HAVEN: Ammon, when are we going?

AMMON: In September.

HAVEN: Raise your hand on this one: How are we traveling there?

CARTER: In the car.

HAVEN: Ammon, who is your favorite Disney character?

AMMON: Minnie Mouse.

HAVEN: Carter, who is your favorite Disney character?

CARTER: Donald and Goofy.

HAVEN: Ammon, why is Minnie Mouse your favorite character?

AMMON: Because she plants flowers at Mickey's Clubhouse.

HAVEN: Carter, why are Goofy and Donald Duck your favorite characters?

CARTER: Because they're silly!

HAVEN: When we are in Disney World at the resort, what are we going to be doing once a day with some of the characters?

BOTH: Eat with them!

HAVEN: We are! We have some sit-down character dinners. When we're at the Hollywood studios, Ammon, which of the characters we've discussed—Jake, June, or Agent Oso—would you like to eat with?

AMMON: June. I like the way she sings and dances.

HAVEN: Carter, which character would you like to eat with?

CARTER: Jake, because he can do what Captain Hook can't do and he does helpful things.

For those readers who are non-parents or non-kids, June is a character from Disney's *Little Einsteins*, Jake is a Neverland pirate, and Special Agent Oso is a teddy bear who is the lead character is an animated series of the same name.

As a professional educator, Haven has taken a conscious approach to using good questioning to guide his children's discovery about people, places, things, and events in time. In his parenting book, he has a chapter on "choosing souvenirs for future learning," and tells a story of how having reindeer souvenirs of a previous trip sparked a series of questions about the difference between reindeer and a white-tailed deer the kids saw. After asking questions such as "Where do they live?" and "What do they eat?" Haven says,

My 4-year-old preschool children had compared and contrasted two species of deer (natural science/zoology). In Bloom's Taxonomy of objectives in learning, Carter and Ammon were working on the 4th tier of his 6-tier pyramid. Going from the base of the pyramid (remembering), where the objectives in learning are easier, to the pinnacle (creating) of the pyramid, where you create with all the things you've learned, the levels are Remembering, Understanding, Applying, Analyzing, Evaluating, and Creating. They were also learning world geography as we found the countries where reindeer lived. How was I engaging my children in this kind of learning? By relying on some souvenirs we had collected during our travels to guide the questioning.[2]

In a real sense, all Haven is doing is advancing the children's natural tendency to ask simple, direct questions. In contrast to this, many adults, including teachers, have a tendency to lead children astray with bad questioning styles. Consider this common exchange:

CHILD: I'm bored.

DAD: Don't you have some books to read?

CHILD: Yes. But I don't feel like reading.

DAD: Would you like to ride your bike?

CHILD: No.

DAD: When I was your age I never got bored, and I didn't have as much as you have. Why don't you clean your room?

CHILD: Then I'd be more bored.

Now let's see the father switch to slightly better questions:

DAD: Really?

CHILD: Yeah, there's nothing to do around here.

DAD: So, what's it feel like to be bored?

CHILD: You know, nothing feels like fun to do.

DAD: How else does it feel to be bored?

CHILD: You know, nothing is happening.

DAD: What do you think we can do to make today not so boring?

CHILD: Go somewhere!

DAD: Where would you like to go?

Toddlers particularly can be masters of persistent questioning, but it's probably not because they intend to annoy you. According to Leon Hoffman, MD, co-director of the Pacella Parent Child Center at the New York Psychoanalytic Society & Institute, they may ask the same question over and over again for at least three reasons. They are trying to:

1. **Understand words.** Children between the ages of 1 and 2 are just learning to talk, so they repeat questions to get clear on what each word means.

2. **Build memory.** Sometimes it takes a little while for new information to sink in to a toddler's developing mind. Hearing a trusted parent give the same answers time and again can help drive unfamiliar concepts home.

3. **Check in.** Because toddlers find comfort in repetition, rewinding and replaying questions is just a way of asking for emotional support.[3]

Two of the three reasons, therefore, are actually a type of discovery. Don't discourage your toddler from persistent questioning—she may be on her way to becoming a doctor.

SOCIAL QUESTIONING

Susan RoAne, aka The Mingling Maven, offers keen advice on the nature and use of questions in a social situation. In her book *What Do I Say Next?*, she devotes several sections to what conversation is *not*. "Conversation is not a soliloquy" is one piece of advice, which she precedes by telling a pointed story of a colleague who told her quite confidently that, even though RoAne had written the (best-selling) book *How to Work a Room*, that *he* really knew how to work a room. In fact, he was so good at it that when he left a room, people who remained in it felt a void. RoAne correctly assessed that they welcomed the void. She and her friend Jeanie had encountered him at an event where he had immediately launched into a 10-minute update on his life and recent achievements. And then he walked away:

> Gary never asked a question of either of us, and made no attempt at anything that resembled a conversation. Jeanie had a client in his field, which she happened to mention at one point. If he had shut his mouth and listened, he would not have blown this lead from her. I had mentioned that I was writing this book, giving him a topic to bounce off of, but he lacked the *interest* to inquire about it.[4]

The incident triggered a recollection that RoAne had of a colleague's "Five-Minute Rule": If a person you're speaking with does not ask a question in the first five minutes, it's time to leave.

DATING AND QUESTIONING

Building on RoAne's "Five-Minute Rule," if you are on a date and the other person asks no questions about you, you could walk away—or you could dismiss the faux pas as the nervousness associated with a date trying to impress you or amuse you. So, I'd say give him/her 10 minutes to start asking you about yourself. There is the opposite problem of course—which RoAne calls a "probe-lem"—and that is the situation in which the date acts like an interrogator. A barrage of "Where did you go to school?" "What's your sign?" and "Who did you vote for?" is the stuff of a bad date, no matter how attractive the person it.

The nature of your questions on a date speaks volumes about what you're genuinely looking for a in a companion, as well as what you have to offer. Keeping the conversation focused on skiing or going to parties suggests you want a playmate. Questions about the future suggest you want a wedding. ASAP.

Here's a story that illustrates the importance of asking the right questions. Paul and Ann met on her first day at the office; her cubicle was next to his. They had an immediate attraction and he asked her out before the day was over. Ann is the kind of person who enjoys learning about what makes a person tick. Her questions on their first date kept them talking almost all night about every thing from favorite novels to space travel.

Three months later, their relationship still held magic for both of them and they started talking about moving in together. And then, one of his former girlfriends showed up at work and took him to lunch. They came back two hours later, with the girlfriend showing signs of having had too much Chianti with her pasta. Leaning into Ann's cube, she said in a snarky tone, "His mother won't like you either," and then she swayed toward the exit.

Later that night, when Ann and Paul were together, she asked why the girlfriend had said that. Paul explained that he'd never had a girlfriend his mother did not think was a gold-digger. In all those three months, Ann had never asked Paul about his background because she figured he would talk about it if he wanted to. Instead she got to know him inside, never finding out that his mother came from an enormously wealthy family.

"Don't worry, Ann," he said to her. "There are lots of reasons why she won't come to that conclusion about you." The story had a happy ending.

PERSONAL QUESTIONS AND PERSONALITY

Anyone can be trained to ask good questions, and even people who are reticent to ask questions can generally do it comfortably in a professional setting. In a social or personal situation, it can be a very different matter, however.

You may be predisposed to ask questions about feeling and values—"What can we do about puppy mills?" Or, you may be inclined to ask questions that essentially render an opinion or some sense of how you think the question should be answered—"Why do you think Congress has been foot-dragging on immigration reform?" I think the Myers-Briggs Type Indicator (MBTI) is a useful tool to provide insights on how a person might be predisposed to approaching questioning. Understanding your predominant type and that of people you interact with often could improve your questioning and listening. Ann's approach to questions with Paul captures exactly who she is in terms of the MBTI: Introvert, Intuitive, Feeling, Perceiving. Princess Diana is considered a famous example of an INFP. On the Myers-Briggs Website (*www.myersbriggs.org*), INFPs are described as:

> Idealistic, loyal to their values and to people who are important to them. Want an external life that is congruent with their values. Curious, quick to see possibilities, can be catalysts for implementing ideas. Seek to understand people and to help them fulfill their potential. Adaptable, flexible, and accepting unless a value is threatened.[5]

In considering the characteristics of the various types summarized by the following grid, I concluded that the "judgers" were probably least likely to ask open-ended questions. The Js are those "who prefer to get things decided," as opposed to the perceivers, who "prefer to stay open to new information and options." Most of us tend to wiggle from one block to another, depending on context, so there is no absolute associated with this view of who makes a good questioner.

ISTJ	ISFJ	INFJ	INTJ
ISTP	ISFP	INFP	INTP
ESTP	ESFP	ENFP	ENTP
ESTJ	ESFJ	ENFJ	ENTJ

In considering which types might be better than others in blatant lies, inconsistencies, and evasions, I would turn again to *How to Spot a Liar*, which analyzes the possibilities according to temperament types. Based on Myers-Briggs profiles, the temperament types are: rationals, idealists, artisans, and guardians. They were first categorized as such by David Kiersey and Marilyn Bates in their book *Please Understand Me*. In brief, rationals are primarily characterized by a combination of intuiting and thinking. Senior military leaders and CEOs would likely fall into this category. With people like that in mind, you might assume they are good liars; in fact, they don't lie well because they are not accustomed to thinking that they need to lie. Idealists, who combine intuition and feeling, tend to make good liars. They just want everybody to get along, and sometimes, evading the truth is the best way to help make that happen. ("No, you don't look fat in those pants!") Guardians are sensing-judging people who don't tend to lie well. They would try to avoid situations that might involve omitting or sidestepping the truth. The sensing-perceiving artisans "get you in the ballpark of the truth,"[6] according to Deborah Singer Dobson, the expert cited in this section of *How to Spot a Liar.*

QUESTIONING TO KNOW YOURSELF BETTER

You're a character in the reality show you call your life. Just as questions have helped me understand the characters I've created in role-playing situations in training interrogators, I believe they can help you as well. Asking yourself good questions *about yourself* can lead to some wonderful revelations about your motivations, priorities, goals, and so on.

In training intelligence collectors, I had to develop an adversarial persona who was able to answer all of the questions I knew they would ask when I was testing their abilities to gain cooperation and seek information. My process was to envision a person in a particular environment, give him a personal and professional element, and then overlay it with regional culture and language. Some of the roles were very technical and scientific, and all were woven around the personal motivations and vulnerabilities that we all have.

I have been so many different people in the last 25 years that I fear in my old age my brain may call on one of the less friendly characters I've been and lock its memory there. No one in the nursing home will want to sit with me during meals. They'll just say, "Jim Pyle? Oh, that's the mean guy over there. You won't want to talk to him!"

My students have had to question me as a foreign soldier, a sailor, an airman, a drug courier, a suicide bomber, a terrorist cell leader, and an ex-patriot with information on a foreign government's nuclear, political, or military plans. Some roles were simple and easy to exploit whereas others contained layers and nuances not easily detected or exploited. For many students, finding out what I knew about research into the effects of high-frequency pulse radiation and its effects on the hippo-campus of the brain was a little more involved than why, as a disenfranchised young man from a poor village, I was willing to carry drugs across the border so my family could eat.

Discovery questioning proved quite helpful as I developed roles for the students to question. It's straight-forward: If the information students are going to acquire is the result of asking questions, then the process of building a role begins with questions. It follows exactly as discovery questioning should: a basic question with the necessary follow-up in all the areas of people, places, things, and events in time.

In the case of my identity as Eduardo Morales, I was a lone individual who emerged from the bulrushes along the beach near Guantanamo Bay, Cuba, with nothing more than a diver's knife and 500 pesos, wearing a modern U.S. military life jacket. I became Eduardo by asking myself questions: Who am I? Who makes up my family? Who are my friends? Where did I come from? What was my job? What schooling did I have? How did I get to this place? Why did I come to this place? Eduardo was built by questions and he was revealed by questions. In other words, he came apart the same way he was constructed.

If I were going to play *you* in such an exercise, what questions would I need to answer so that I could get away with it?

EXERCISE

Keep a journal for two weeks related to questions in your personal life. If you are keeping the Monday-through-Friday journal as suggested in the previous chapter, then you could just focus this journal on evenings and weekends.

Begin by making notes in three areas of your past questioning:

1. List five questions you asked that made a difference in your personal life. Put a short notation as to why you feel each served you well.

2. Add five questions you wish you had never posed. When it comes to your personal life, you may have some anxiety over these questions, so don't bother to make a notation on why you have a tinge of regret about asking them. No need to rub salt in the wound.

3. Add five questions you believe you should have asked differently.

   ✗ How do you wish you would have stated the question?

   ✗ How would restating the question have potentially changed the answer you got?

In your journal, keep notes about how the structure, placement, frequency, and other pertinent factors related to your questions has changed.

1. Record one question each day that made a difference in terms of a personal relationship. (Note: You might have asked a question that threw someone into a state of rage. That counts as making a difference.)

2. Record one question you wish you hadn't posed. (If none, then congratulations.)

3. Record one question you think would have gotten a better answer if asked a different way. (If none, then you're probably kidding yourself.)

   ✗ How do you wish you would have stated the question?

   ✗ How would restating the question have potentially changed the answer you got?

Chapter 9

. . . .

Fast-Track to Expertise

In Rain Man, *Raymond Babbit (Dustin Hoffman) amazes his brother Charlie (Tom Cruise) by memorizing the alphanumeric designations of all the songs on a table-top diner jukebox in minutes. Charlie reads the name of the song; Raymond shoots back "G4," "M1," and so on. What's Raymond's strategy for convincing his brother that he's an expert? None. He doesn't even know what an expert is.*

—Gregory Hartley, *How to Become an Expert on Anything in 2 Hours*

Expertise reflects a deliberate effort by someone to project knowledge. For example, Maryann grew up in a town where Bethlehem Steel Corporation had an important presence. She had a lot of anecdotal information about plant operations, executive decisions, and financial problems, but mere exposure to information does not make one an expert in a subject—otherwise almost everyone would be an expert on sex and food. It wasn't until Maryann researched Bethlehem Steel for an in-depth piece about the causes of the company's bankruptcy that she approached having any expertise about the company or its industry. She made a concerted effort to learn, applied her background to analyzing the information, and created a package of lessons about the company's failure for the benefit of other business executives.

Expertise is also defined by the listener. For example, I know a lot about how to build a racing car and could pour facts into your ear for a few hours, but if you don't see how that information applies to your life then I did not demonstrate expertise. All I did was demonstrate an encyclopedic knowledge of engines, aerodynamics, and other subjects related to fast cars—but you could have gotten the same information from Wikipedia. Does that make Wikipedia an expert?

VETTING THE SOURCE

Whom do you think of as an expert? Why do you think that person is an expert? When Maryann and I were composing the chapter on questioning in professions, we looked to people who are in the professions of education, medicine, emergency response, law, and customer service, and we cited a source that had actually conducted a successful business negotiation. Having such credentialed experts in those areas contribute thoughts to the book ensured that our guidance on questioning was grounded in reality. I have a lot of experience using questions in interrogations and sales situations, but I wanted to know how an actual M.D. asked questions, and why he or she did it that way. My theoretical knowledge of how to question in a clinical environment lacks gravitas. And in the chapter on "questioning in your personal life," we had profiles in mind of people who would be good sources of guidance on using questions, specifically a doctor of education who is also a parent, and an author/speaker who is well-known for her expertise in social networking.

The process of selecting a qualified human source is relatively simple. The process of determining how much of an expert the source is can be complicated:

✗ **Find a source associated with the subject.** People who know me and Greg Hartley from the interrogation arena might assume that I have the same level of expertise that he does in reading and using body language, but I don't. If you want to know something about body language, go to him, not to me—although, if you do come to me, my expertise at that moment is in directing you to the person you ought to be talking to. Therefore, sometimes this step has to be repeated, as in:

"What do you know about body language, Jim?"

"I know enough to know I'm not an expert. But my friend Greg is."

"How do I find him?"

✗ **Make sure the source is accessible.** If you want investment advice, if would be great if you could pick up the phone and call Warren Buffet. If you want insights on playing the cello, you could try to make an appointment with Yo Yo Ma. Good luck on both counts. The source is no good if you can't pose the questions to him.

✗ **Cross-check the source** if there is any hint of doubt about the quality of answers you received. For example, Maryann wanted to make a passing reference to a phenomenon in physics, but wasn't quite sure how to do an efficient online search for the information, so she called an old friend who had studied physics in college. "Hey, David," she asked, "what's that term in physics that describes the phenomenon that occurs when two people are holding hands and bouncing on a trampoline, hitting and peaking at the same time, but then they break their grasp and starting hitting at different times so they wind up with completely opposite rhythm?" I'm not going to comment on the structure of her question, but it did get an answer that she was able to search online. He said, "I studied physics in college and I've been a CPA ever since, so check me on this, but I think you're talking about amplitude oscillations."

✗ **If you query a search engine** rather than a person about a subject, you input keywords and don't bother with non-searchable words like "the" or "and." In asking a person who has information, and possibly expertise, about a subject it's important to keep that model in mind. You wouldn't ask a search engine, "Do you think a sharknado could ever really happen?" if you wanted to know whether or not it's possible that a storm could flood Los Angeles with shark-infested water. You would input something like "real life sharknado." So if your source were a meteorologist, you would begin with that core phrase and ask, "What are the conditions that might cause a real-life sharknado?" Remember to start with what you know, determine what you don't know, and then shape your questions accordingly.

QUESTIONING LIKE A SKEPTIC

If you believe everything you hear, then you won't be an expert in anything but blind faith. Conspiracy theories provide the perfect occasion to test your questioning skills and how they support the development of expertise. With the four discovery areas in mind, put together a list of questions you would ask someone who told you the following story:

President Franklin Roosevelt provoked the Japanese attack on the U.S. naval base in Hawaii on December 7, 1941. He knew all about it in advance and covered up his failure to warn his fleet commanders. There's evidence that he needed the attack to provoke Adolf Hitler into declaring war on the United States because the American people and Members of Congress were overwhelmingly against entering the war in Europe.

The United States received warnings from Britain, the Netherlands, Australia, Peru, Korea, and the Soviet Union that a surprise attack on Pearl Harbor was coming. In addition, the U.S. military had intercepted and broken all the important Japanese codes in the run-up to the attack, so Americans had the intelligence on the Japanese plan.

If I were putting questions together, I would start with information I have already learned about the attack. It's my baseline; that is, my basis for evaluating other things I hear about the subject. I learned things in various schools, from elementary through military. Much of that material doesn't really address the core premise of the conspiracy theory, though. Probably the most salient body of information I had exposure to was Roberta Wohlstetter's 1962 book *Pearl Harbor: Warning and Decision.* Wohlstetter, who was a preeminent historian of American military intelligence, determined that it wasn't a failure of American intelligence that led to the attack, nor was it a disregard for the intelligence the United States had about Japan. She calls it a "failure of imagination"; the United States just didn't believe Japan could or would bomb U.S. territory.

With Wohlstetter as my lead source, therefore, I would begin my questioning with, "Who is your source of the information?" The question, "What evidence does your source have?" would follow it. Keep in mind that with a conspiracy theory, the two people debating it are most likely not the people who have primary source material to support their points of view. The questions need to loop back to who the source is and what evidence the source has of the timeline, locations, key figures, and events related to the story.

QUESTIONING LIKE AN ANALYST

Practice is the best way to sharpen your evolving expertise as a questioner. One of my favorite expertise-sharpening exercises with students used to be "Interrogate the Newspaper." I've updated my vocabulary in recent years and now it's called "Interrogate the News Source," as I'm one of many people who gets my news online.

Journalism is the embodiment of discovery questioning. Guided by *who, what, when, where,* and *why,* a professional conveying the news tries to put the most important information first, and pertinent supporting information immediately after that. Bringing to bear your new questioning skills, you can evaluate whether or not they succeed; you now have a better sense than before of what questions need to be asked based on the four discovery areas. You don't have to depend on the accuracy of a slogan like "Fair and Balanced" or "All the news that's fit to click." You can decide for yourself.

To demonstrate how to apply your skills to interrogating a news source, I'm going to analyze a key news story from 2012. First of all, regardless of whether the story is in print or online, a grabber headline rivets the reader's attention. The headline for the lead article in *The Day* of New London, Connecticut, for December 15, 2012, reads simply, "Unthinkable." It covers the tragic shooting at Sandy Hook Elementary School.

Seeing just the headline, I begin my questioning and let the newspaper "answer" me:

What is unthinkable?	The shooting and death of schoolchildren
Who else was shot?	Adults at the school
Who else was shot?	The shooter's mother
Who else was shot?	The shooter
Where did the shooting take place?	Newtown, Connecticut
Where, exactly?	Sandy Hook Elementary School
How many children were shot and killed?	20
How many adults were killed?	7

When did the shooting occur?	December 14, 2012
When exactly did it occur?	9 a.m.
Who shot the children?	Adam Lanza
Who is Adam Lanza?	The 20-year-old son of Nancy Lanza, who was also killed prior to the massacre
Why did he shoot the children?	Unknown

Many questions would follow, of course, about what he used to shoot them, how many people were wounded, and so on. But if you reverse engineer this exercise, you can envision a reporter asking a law enforcement officer or other official on the scene these very questions to arrive at a lead paragraph such as the following:

At 9:00 on Friday, December 14, 20-year-old Adam Lanza opened fire at Sandy Hook Elementary School in Newtown, Connecticut, killing 20 schoolchildren and five adults on the scene before killing himself. He is the son of Nancy Lanza, found dead in her home, presumably also killed by her son. Lanza's motive for the massacre is unknown.

In the confusion and trauma of a scene like this one, it would be easy for a journalist to hear the cries of "why?" and "how?" overwhelming the questions that must form the core of good reporting. It would also be tempting to draw from eyewitness accounts, which may actually reflect flawed memory and speculation, into the story and present them as fact. Anyone who doubts that reporting the news requires skill, focus, and judgment should consider how difficult it would be to accurately report the story of Sandy Hook immediately after it occurred.

Whether you get your news from reading or listening, interrogate the source to sharpen your expertise as a questioner.

QUESTIONING LIKE AN INTELLIGENCE OFFICER

The fundamental skill is to maintain subject focus while developing leads to gain additional, relevant details.

I've always said, if I can see it, I can do it. I have to see it to mimic it before I can master it, and so for those of you who, like me, benefit from a map to stay on subject, I offer three ways to depict the flow of a conversation from point of inquiry to discovery. Learning to ask the next best question based on the response to the previous question sometimes involves seeing what questions take you off track.

The first representation is a typical maze. The following interchange could start with the original query and dead-end quickly by having the questioner follow up with either question 1 or question 2. However, if the questioner continues on a path of logical discovery, she finds herself at the other end of the maze.

Original query (a good question, properly framed):

QUESTION: Jim, I understand you are the inventor of the Electronic Language Simulator (ELS). What made you think of a device to assist Human Intelligence Collectors working with interpreters?

ANSWER: In business, making money is one of the first concerns.

Next question:

1. How much money? (not aligned with the initial question)

2. What is a good business model for training? (not aligned with the initial question)

3. **What else besides money made you want to invent a device to assist training?** (the best follow-up to the initial question)

ANSWER: The other key objective I can think of is supporting staffing requirements. In order to train anyone using an interpreter, you need not one but two individuals that speak a language uncommon to the primary questioner.

Next question:

1. What languages are most popular to train with? (not aligned with the initial question)

2. What language does the questioner speak? (not aligned with the initial question)

3. **Why do you need two individuals?** (the best follow-up to the initial question)

ANSWER: You need one to play a role speaking only in the uncommon language and another who can speak as the interpreter in both the common (English in this case) and the uncommon language.

Next question:

1. How do you determine what is and what is not a common/uncommon language? (not aligned with the initial question and a poorly phrased compound question)

2. Can you tell me a little more about how the role-players are supposed to act? (not aligned with the initial question and a poorly phrased question)

3. **How is "two individuals" a staffing problem?** (the best follow-up to the initial question)

ANSWER: It is very difficult to find the required number of certified linguists at the same proficiency level.

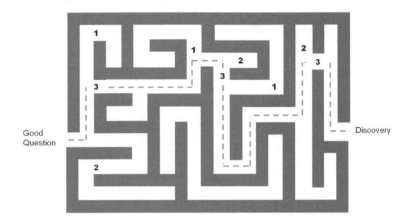

Good
Question

Discovery

The second representation is a flow chart. The interchange starts with the original query, with arrows indicating the best, next question to come to a point of discovery and pinpointing expertise:

Original query (a good question, properly framed): Jim, I understand you are the inventor of the Electronic Language Simulator (ELS). What made you think of a device to assist Human Intelligence Collectors (HIC) working with interpreters?

ANSWER: HIC students at our Alexandria Virginia Training Facility asked for more interpreter training. ["HIC students" should be noted for additional questioning in the "people" area; "Alexandria Training Center" should be noted for additional questioning in the "place" area.]

Is training in the use of interpreters a difficult subject?	What interpreter training had they received? ⬇	Who teaches interpreter training?
	A two-hour demonstration of the interaction and placement of interpreters.	
What kind of training did they want? ⬇	Isn't a two-hour demonstration enough?	Where is the best place to seat an interpreter?
They wanted certified linguists to play the adversarial and interpreter roles during training exercises.		

Are certified linguists hard to find?	What do you do during your training exercises?	What was the training center response to that request?
		⬇ *From a business standpoint, there was more than one reason not to fulfill that student request.*
Does the business model always drive the train at the center?	What is one of the reasons it was a business challenge?	Why do students think they can direct the training?
	⬇ *In business, cost and reasonable profit are always concerns.*	

What is a good cost-to-profit margin?	What's reasonable?	What else? ⬇
		It is very difficult to find the required number of certified linguists at the same proficiency level.
How do you certify a linguist?	Who maintains a stable of linguists?	What else? ⬇
		Those were the two reasons it was prohibitive.

		Given that cost and limited staffing were problems, what exactly was the cost problem?
		Certified linguist role-players command as much as three times the per-hour contract than non-linguist role players.
		Really!

		On top of that, you require two per student per training exercise, so with 12 students and 10 four-hour training exercises, it was absolutely cost prohibitive.

At this point, the flow goes directly to an explanation of how the ELS enabled the Alexandria Training Center to meet the students' request in an affordable and effective way.

The third representation (shown on the following page) is a graphic created by Greg Hartley for *How to Spot a Liar*. This "questioning chart" focuses on following a source lead.

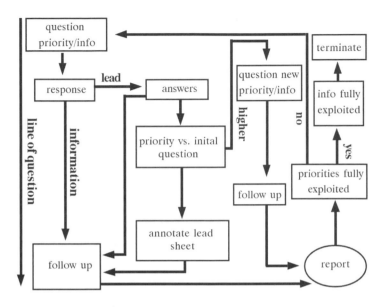

The response to a question provides either information or a lead. The lead meets a priority need or an information requirement, or it dead ends. Follow the lead; determine whether or not it yields something of higher importance than the initial question. If it yields lower-importance information, make a note, and go back to follow up on the original question. If higher, follow that line of questioning. At some point, you have followed up on all leads and information; terminate the questioning. If you haven't fully exploited what the person knows, return to the beginning.[1]

MATCHING INTERESTS
WITH KNOWLEDGE

The personal relevance of expertise is a game-changer in terms of how well people listen to you, what they do with the information you give them, and how the shared information affects their relationship with you. In teaching questioning skills to Special Forces and Navy SEALS, I saw they had passion for honing any skill set that would help them perform better. When I walked into the training, they had been told I could deliver, and their intent was to leave the training as good as I was or better. When the expert and the desire for his or her expertise converge in this manner, transformations occur in professional and personal lives. This is the foundation for the success of the truly knowledgeable and gifted self-help gurus.

The phenomenon can occur in some seemingly ordinary ways that are nonetheless important. Here is an example of a first encounter between Bob, a former Navy pilot and avid boater, and his daughter's boyfriend, who is an accomplished skydiver. Bob doesn't expect to find much in common with this daredevil and secretly wishes his daughter would have stuck with the dentist she had been dating. Bob is a lawyer, and a skilled questioner, so he defaults to a discovery posture. The boyfriend knows that Bob is a former pilot and enjoys motoring around the Chesapeake Bay in his boat. He knows if he doesn't find some way to connect on those major interests, the girlfriend—despite the fact that she's a grown woman—will have an uphill battle in getting her dad's approval:

Bob: Do I understand correctly that you have five world records?

Jim: Yes. They are skydiving world records. Three for the largest skydiving formations ever built, and two for the largest jump with two distinct formations.

Bob: I don't quite get it. What are the last two?

Jim: Two different, distinct formations. No group had even done them with that many people before.

Bob: Wow! So what's a formation?

Jim: Skydiving formations are simply a group of skydivers that are arrayed in the air in freefall in a pre-determined pattern.

Bob: And how do you make that pattern?

Jim: It's a matter of whatever design has been created by the people who are organizing the jump.

Bob: But how do you make the pattern?

Jim: On the ground, on paper, or in the air?

Bob: In the air!

Jim: In the air, it's a matter of the skydivers all coming to a central point to their prescribed positions, maneuvering their bodies in freefall such that they join the formation where they're supposed to.

Bob: How do you maneuver?

JIM: The human body has control services just like an aircraft—your arms, and your legs, and your torso—and there are various ways you can manipulate them to affect where you go.

BOB: Oh! So parts of your body become directional control surfaces like rudders.

JIM: Exactly. You can be precise in directing yourself to a location if you have the skill.

Bob is now engaged. This is more than a conversation to find out what his daughter's boyfriend does. They are starting to speak the same language.

BOB: How do you attach yourself to the people you're maneuvering toward?

JIM: You use the only thing you have available to you, which is your hands.

The conversation continued with a discussion of fall rate and other factors that really piqued Bob's curiosity, such as planning a large-formation skydive. Bob's points of reference were filing a flight plan, flying in a pattern, and making mechanical adjustments to compensate for cross-winds and other environmental factors. Most important in this social situation, the discussion helped him understand how his knowledge as a pilot, and to some extent, a boater, intersected with Jim's expertise as a skydiver. When they got into a discussion of threatening situations, Bob asked:

BOB: What's the most dangerous situation you've ever been in?

JIM: A near canopy collision a few times. Right after opening, I found myself heading toward someone else whose canopy had just opened.

BOB: How did you avert the danger?

JIM: There's a standard response that we are trained to have. Both parties turn right. It's a process that, if executed promptly, averts the problem.[2]

This is another point at which the skydiving expertise intersects with the interests and experience of people in boating and flying: averting danger by knowing what side you're on or what to do if you're coming at someone head-on is critical. When Bob's daughter asked him what he thought of her new boyfriend, he said, "Jim and I have a lot in common."

PREPARE FOR SURPRISES

Your enhanced questioning and listening skills will no doubt help you discover expertise in places you didn't know it existed. It may not happen quickly, however, and it may not happen as predictably as you would like.

Two of the most useful pieces of advice I ever got about the patience, listening, and rapport-building that I would need with sources were from a mentor of mine in my early days as an interrogator. The first was "Watch *Seinfeld*." The sitcom that aired from 1989 to 1998 was notoriously about "nothing." My mentor said, "They talk a lot about nothing before they get to the good stuff." The second piece of advice was, "Watch the food channel," because, "No matter who the source is, if you can talk about food you have something in common."

Eric Maddox's dramatic story of the capture of Saddam Hussein involved a lot of moments that were not dramatic. In fact, there were a good many conversations with sources that seemed to be about nothing—and many of them involved food. Maddox rightly figured that if he could painstakingly find his way to the people and the fishing hole that enabled Saddam Hussein to have his favorite dish on a regular basis, he would find his target. He asked the questions that took him to the expert who prepared masgoof for the dictator.

Ask good questions and prepare for surprises.

Conclusion

· ·

On a quiet hillside in Forest Lawn Memorial Park in Los Angeles I conducted the memorial service for my brother Richard—the one who shared my sense of discovery with the 1956 Buick we tore apart when we were kids. It seemed as though my whole being was consumed by questions on that hillside, some of which didn't have answers.

At that moment, it occurred to me that discovery had became a way of life at an early age. My impulse to question and learn, and my desire to hear other people engage in discovery, was partly to blame for my setting aside a career as a preacher. The other part was money—you have to make a living, of course, so I took my unbridled curiosity and applied it sales, where it was both a good fit and a profitable one. When I sold peace of mind associated with the real estate at Forest Lawn—we didn't say we sold cemetery plots or crypts—my good questions meant good information, and good information meant sales.

Ever since then, it seems I've made my living asking questions, including investing 20 years in military service and further developing, employing, and ultimately teaching the skills you have learned in this book.

The only way I have ever known if I did a good job in teaching these skills is to detect "aha!" moments in my students. It's the moment when I see they have integrated the material into their psyche. It's when I hear a leading or yes/no question start to come out of their mouths—"Do you..." —and then a pause and a correction. Where "Do you" stood before, an interrogative has taken its place: "What do you..." A better question gets put in play immediately. I trust this has at least started to happen to you.

As a mnemonic device to reinforce the critical elements of good questioning, I came up with the following equation:

$$2 + 6 \text{ over } F \times 4 = \text{Good Questioning}$$

The parts mean this:

✗ Question with the curiosity of a 2-year-old.

✗ Use the six interrogatives—*who, what, when, where, why,* and *how* (and sometimes "huh?").

✗ Lay that on top of follow-up.

✗ Make sure to cover all four of the discovery areas: people, places, things, and events in time.

The result is efficient, effective, precise, and complete questioning, which translates into "good questioning."

I wanted to conclude with some of the greatest questions ever posed. They're great because they start with an interrogative, require a narrative response, and are likely to be questions you remember for the rest of your life. That's a tall order!

So, for all of those who are kindred spirits in discovery, who deeply appreciate the learning value of a great question, here are my top 10. (I'm going to do this like David Letterman and go from 10 to 1, which is my favorite.)

10. Why was I born?

9. What is life?

8. What is death?

7. What is reality?

6. Where is heaven?

5. When will I feel satisfied?

4. Whom can I trust?

3. How do I know if I'm really in love?

2. How do I know if someone really loves me?

1. What would happen if...?

Appendix

· ·

Supplemental Exercises to Sharpen Questioning Skills

WHAT DO YOU KNOW THAT I DON'T KNOW THAT I WOULDN'T KNOW IF I DIDN'T ASK?

or

UNCOVERING EXPERTISE

After interrogation students complete the blocks of instruction in questioning, the first exercise I give them is to uncover expertise. The crazy question that serves as the title of this exercise is one way of asking someone, "What do you consider yourself an expert about?" If you ask me the question, I will respond with, "The Indy 500, Forest Lawn Memorial Park in Los Angeles, and Merle Haggard." It would then be up to you to see how much you could pull out of me on one of those three subjects by using interrogatives. It would also be your task to challenge my familiarity with the subject. My job is to give complete, narrative responses to any good questions, but not tell you more than you asked.

To do the exercise:

1. Get a partner (you could also do this with a group).

2. Have everyone list subjects about which they consider themselves deeply knowledgeable. If anyone lists more than three, that person may be the perfect target to hit first, because there aren't many people who can claim to be a painter, sculptor, architect, musician, mathematician, engineer, inventor, anatomist, geologist, cartographer, botanist, and writer like Leonardo DaVinci.

3. Ask only discovery questions—that is, questions that begin with one of the six interrogatives—and see how much you can find out about the subject you've chosen in five minutes.

4. The "expert" may only answer the question asked. He or she may not volunteer any additional information.

5. Be curious. Ask follow-up questions in the four discovery areas.

At the end of the exercise, if you haven't gained any great revelations about the subject—if, in fact, what you've been told by the supposed expert is either common knowledge or speculation—then you've successfully challenged the person's familiarity with the subject. On the other hand, if you are exclaiming, "Really?" and "Wow" within five minutes, then you've succeeded in uncovering expertise.

After you do this with friends, family, and coworkers, then take your skill to the streets. Do the exercise with perfect strangers who have no idea why you are so curious about what they know.

This is a practical exercise with people who are trying to sell you something, by the way. How deep is their product knowledge? It's also a great way to vet someone offering to provide you services—consulting, surgery, legal representation, or anything else in which you expect the provider to have a high level of expertise.

ONE-A-DAY CHALLENGE

In this exercise, your aim is to select a subject that you know nothing about and find out as much as possible in roughly five minutes using a human source. Do it every day. This is similar to the first exercise, but you are not laying any restrictions on the respondent in terms of whether or not the person answers your question precisely. Also, it's not a team exercise; it's a personal one designed to sharpen your questioning skills while you learn something new.

This exercise ties in well with the following one.

ADVANCED JOURNALING

In Chapters 7 and 8, I introduced the concept of journaling and provided descriptions of what journal entries to make to improve your questioning in both your professional and your personal list. Without reiterating the portion of the exercise that helps you start the journal—the list of items that require some reflection on your past—I want to add a few items to the list of what you could do going forward.

Here is the list as recommended in the chapters:

1. Record one question each day that made a difference in terms of getting something done at work or made a difference in terms of a personal relationship.

2. Record one question you wish you hadn't posed. (If none, then congratulations.)

3. Record one question you think would have gotten a better answer if asked a different way. (If none, then you're probably kidding yourself.)

   ✗ How do you wish you would have stated the question?

   ✗ How would restating the question have potentially changed the answer you got?

Here are items to add to do advanced journaling:

✗ Record the best question of the day. It could have been something someone said to you directly, or something you heard on TV or read online. Why did you think it was the best?

✗ Same thing for the worst question of the day.

It's up to you if you want to be a bully with this journaling exercise. I have unpleasant visions of people whipping out their journals in the middle of a meeting and shouting, "That's the worst question I've heard all day, and it's going in my book!"

DIDN'T ASK, DON'T TELL!

For role-players in questioning scenarios for military Human Intelligence Collection, the watchwords for cooperation were "believable approach" and "good questioning technique." The reward for abiding by them would be the information that the questioner asked for. On the other hand, if the student's performance was less than believable and the questioning was not well structured and organized, the information he got was very limited, and we withheld it until we saw improved performance. I would instruct the role players—actors who took on the persona and operational activity of insurgents, terrorists, or individuals with specialized knowledge—to answer only if the question was well phrased, and not to offer more information than what was requested.

Put yourself in my role-player's position and listen carefully to all questions posed to you; provide only the information requested. It's probably best to do this at a trade-show reception or other event populated by strangers, because if you stick to the rules, you aggravate people. The learning experience will be tremendous, however. By providing only the information requested, you will have firsthand exposure to the degree to which most people depend on your offering more than what was asked in order to get the information they wanted.

I have a stance that I take seriously, and that is "They didn't ask, so I don't tell."

SIX DEGREES OF SEPARATION

This is an exercise I'm adapting from one that Greg Hartley and Maryann described in *How to Become an Expert on Anything in 2 Hours.* The premise is that everyone on Earth is, by association, only six people away from everyone else. So the challenge here is to tie two seemingly unrelated topics together in six questions or fewer.

For example, the person you are talking with is focused on the shaky state of the U.S. economy. You want to talk about the singer/songwriter Taylor Swift. You start questioning:

Where are people suffering most from economic problems?

The respondent gives a sense of people in both rural and urban settings that are having difficulty finding work.

What cities have been hit hardest?

The respondent names some, including Detroit, Michigan, and Reading, Pennsylvania. The former had to declare bankruptcy and the latter has the highest recorded poverty rate in the nation according to the most recent census.

You can actually stop with two questions on this one: Taylor Swift was born in Reading.

You can make people aware of the exercise, or you can simply use your questioning skills to turn a conversation toward something you want to talk about.

Notes

● ●

INTRODUCTION

1. Brooklyn Decker's Twitter account, @ BrooklynDecker, 7:55 p.m., June 23, 2013.

2. Ed Henry, Fox News Chief White House Correspondent, April 30, 2012 Press Conference with President Barack Obama; *www.politico. com/story/2013/04/obama-press-conference- syria-sequestration-transcript-video-90775. html#ixzz2XctIaijr.*

3. Ibid.

4. Ibid.

5. Jessica Yellin, CNN Chief White House Correspondent, April 30, 2012 Press Conference with President Barack Obama; *www.politico. com/story/2013/04/obama-press-conference-syria-sequestration-transcript-video-90775. html#ixzz2XctIaijr.*

6. Ibid.

7. Jonathan Karl, ABC News Chief White House Correspondent, April 30, 2012 Press Conference with President Barack Obama; *www.politico. com/story/2013/04/obama-press-conference-syria-sequestration-transcript-video-90775. html#ixzz2XctIaijr.*

CHAPTER 1

1. Recorded conversations with Judith Bailey, June 25–28, 2013.

2. Michael S. Dobson, "Eyewitness to Murder," Sidewise Thinking blog, April 13, 2010; *sidewiseinsights.blogspot.com/2010/04/ eyewitness-to-murder.html.*

3. *Jeopardy*, July 23, 2004. Ken Jennings won more than any previous contestant.

4. *Jeopardy*, July 8, 2010. Wolf Blitzer, host of CNN's *Situation Room*, managed to sink to a loss of $4,600 in just the first round.

CHAPTER 2

1. "Ayn Rand Mike Wallace Interview 1959, Part 1," *PBS Newshour*; *www.pbs.org/newshour/bb/media/jan-june12/mikewallace_04-09.html*.

2. Mike Wallace, excerpted from "Remembering Mike Wallace, Legendary '60 Minutes' Interrogator," *PBS Newshour*, April 9, 2012; *www.pbs.org/newshour/bb/media/jan-june12/mikewallace_04-09.html*.

3. "Barbra Streisand crying—Mike Wallace Interview—1991—Part 2," YouTube.com; *www.youtube.com/watch?v=-q3rf0d_biQ*.

4. Mike Wallace, excerpted from "Remembering Mike Wallace, Legendary '60 Minutes' Interrogator," *PBS Newshour*, April 9, 2012; *www.pbs.org/newshour/bb/media/jan-june12/mikewallace_04-09.html*.

5. "David Letterman—Borat (Full Interview) HD," YouTube.com; *www.youtube.com/watch?v=Sz3PMfADPdQ*.

6. "Stephen King on Growing Up, Believing in God and Getting Scared," NPR *Fresh Air*, May 28, 2013; *www.npr.org/templates/transcript/transcript.php?storyId=184827647*.

7. "Gene Simmons NPR Interview," YouTube.com; *www.youtube.com/watch?v=xXMpo6rrUcI*.

8. Politi, Daniel. "Fox News to Scholar: Why Would a Muslim Write a Book About Jesus?," Slate.com;

www.slate.com/blogs/the_slatest/2013/07/28/
*video_fox_news_lauren_green_asks_reza_aslan_*
why_muslim_would_be_interested.html.

CHAPTER 3

1. Eric Maddox, *Mission: Black List #1*, New York: HarperCollins, 2008, p. 203.

2. "F. Lee Bailey—Cross-examination of a witness," YouTube.com; *www.youtube.com/watch?v=gVoIz2zNX9U.*

3. Elizabeth F. Loftus, "Leading questions and the eyewitness report," *Cognitive Psychology* 7, Issue 4 (October 1975): 560–572.

4. Meredith Blake, quoting Michael Specter, in "Jenny McCarthy's hiring as 'View' co-host is matter of contention," *Los Angeles Times*, July 16, 2013.

5. "Practice Negative Questions," ProProfs. com; *www.proprofs.com/quiz-school/story. php?title=Practice-Negative-Questions-1.*

6. Gregory Hartley and Maryann Karinch, *How to Spot a Liar: Why People Don't Tell the Truth... and How You Can Catch Them, Second Edition*, Pompton Plains, N.J.: Career Press, 2012, p. 148.

7. "Best Ever To Tell the Truth Feb 18 1963 Surprise Ending," YouTube.com; *www.youtube. com/watch?v=wIUxOO6k8S8.*

CHAPTER 4

1. Edward T. Reilly, *AMA Business Boot Camp*, New York: AMACOM, 2013, pp. 73–74.

2. "Full Interview: Donald Trump on 'The O'Reilly Factor,'" FoxNews.com; *http://video.foxnews.com/v/4622091/ full-interview-donald-trump-on-the-oreilly-factor/.*

3. Ibid.

CHAPTER 5

1. William Klemm, "What Learning Cursive Does for Your Brain," *Psychology Today*, March 14, 2013; *www.psychologytoday. com/blog/memory-medic/201303/ what-learning-cursive-does-your-brain.*

2. "The Wordsmith's Manual Typewriter," Hammacher Schlemmer; *www.hammacher.com/ Product/82670?cm_cat=ProductSEM&cm_ pla=AdWordsPLA&source=PRODSEM.*

3. "Listen Actively and Take Great Notes," The McGraw Center for Teaching & Learning, Princeton University; *www.princeton.edu/mcgraw/ library/for-students/great-notes/.*

4. Jeff Toister, *Service Failure: The Real Reasons Employees Struggle with Customer Service and What You Can Do About It*, New York: AMACOM, 2013, pp. 114–115.

CHAPTER 6

1. Peter Earnest and Maryann Karinch, *Business Confidential*, New York: AMACOM, 2011, p. 95.

2. John R. "Jack" Schafer, PhD, "Let Their Words Do the Talking," *Psychology Today*, March 6, 2011.

CHAPTER 7

1. Michael Brick, "Building a Better School Day," *Parade*, August 11, 2013, p. 8.

2. Dennie Palmer Wolf, "The Art of Questioning," delivered at the Summer Institute of the College Boards Educational Equality Project, held in Santa Cruz, California, July 9–13, 1986, and reprinted in *Academic Connections* (Winter 1987): 1–7; *www.exploratorium.edu/ifi/resources/workshops/artofquestioning.html*.

3. Lynn Neary interview with Brett Patterson: "Answering The Call: The Lives of 911 Dispatchers," Talk of the Nation/ National Public Radio, March 6, 2013;

www.npr.org/2013/03/06/173636645/
answering-the-call-the-lives-of-911-dispatchers.

4. "Listen to Amanda Berry's frantic 9-1-1 call to police," Cleveland.com, May 6, 2013; *www. cleveland.com/metro/index.ssf/2013/05/listen_to_ amanda_berrys_franti.html.*

5. Andrew Kirell, "LISTEN: Cleveland Kidnapping Hero Charles Ramsey's Incredible 911 Call," May 8, 2013, MediaIte.com; *www.mediaite.com/ online/listen-cleveland-kidnapping-hero-charles-ramseys-incredible-911-call/.*

6. Christopher Shea, "Wrong Answer," *Boston Globe*, September 9, 2007; *www.boston. com/news/globe/ideas/articles/2007/09/09/ wrong_answer/?page=full.*

7. Ibid.

8. National Suicide Prevention Lifeline, PDF from Attachment I, Part IV of the Network Agreement, "Imminent Risk"; *www.suicidepreventionlifeline. org/documents/BestPractices/WEB%20 Lifeline%20Imminent%20Risk%20Policy%20 2011.pdf.*

9. David Newdorf, "The Top 10 Killer Deposition Questions," California Litigation Blog, November 1, 2007; *www.newdorf.com.*

10. Deposition of Adam James in Leach v. Texas Tech, p. 75; *http://s3.amazonaws.com/nytdocs/ docs/522/522.pdf.*

11. Jeff Toister, *Service Failure*, New York: AMACOM, 2013, p. 123.

12. Ibid, pp. 123–124.

13. Henry Blodget, "17 Facts About The Apple Store Profit Machine," *Business Insider*, June 25, 2012; *www.businessinsider.com/ apple-store-facts-2012-6?op=1*.

14. Matt Bruenig, "Profit margins for high-wage retailers," March 25, 2013, MattBruenig. com; *http://mattbruenig.com/2013/03/25/ profit-margins-for-high-wage-retailers/*.

CHAPTER 8

1. "Great Questions," StoryCorps; *http://storycorps. org/great-questions/*.

2. Haven Caylor, Ed.D., *Twin Travels* (tentative title of unpublished manuscript).

3. Vivian Manning-Schaffel, "Why Your Toddler Keeps Asking the Same Questions," *Parenting*; *www.parenting.com/article/ why-your-toddler-keeps-asking-the-same-question*.

4. Susan RoAne, *What Do I Say Next?* New York: Warner Books, 1997, p. 182.

5. "The 16 MBTI Types: INFP," The Myers & Briggs Foundation; *www.myersbriggs.org/my- mbti-personality-type/mbti-basics/the-16-mbti- types.asp#INFP*.

6. Gregory Hartley and Maryann Karinch, *How to Spot a Liar, Second Edition*, Pompton Plains, N.J.: Career Press, 2012, p. 71.

CHAPTER 9

1. Gregory Hartley and Maryann Karinch, *How to Spot a Liar*, Pompton Plains, N.J.: Career Press, 2005, p. 142.

2. From an interview with five-time World-record skydiver Jim McCormick on August 14, 2013.

Glossary

adaptor—A nervous or self-soothing movement like rubbing your fingers together or stroking your neck. A person who may be uncomfortable about asking or answering a question might use an adaptor. It's a sign of stress.

barrier—Using a body part or object to put separation between you and another person. The proverbial "cold shoulder" is a barrier. It suggests stress is present.

baseline—The basis for comparison between what is customary and what is a deviation from customary when observing or listening to someone's response to a question. A person who is usually calm, but has a sudden change in voice or movement in responding to a question, is deviating from baseline. It's a sign of stress.

batoning—Using a body part, generally an arm, to emphasize a point. It is a type of *illustrator* that bears a resemblance to a conductor using a baton. In response to a difficult question, a person might use batoning as part of a denial, or to drive home a point that he thinks is particularly noteworthy.

commentator—A commentator is thorough, giving complete answers—in some cases, overly complete in the sense that you get more than you asked for. A commentator may provide such a multifaceted answer that it could take the questioning in a different direction.

compound question—A question that combines two or more subjects, so you are essentially asking two questions at once. For example, "Are you going home or to the restaurant?"

control question—A question to which you already know the answer.

corrective questions—A question your mom, your first grade teacher, or your boss might have asked: "Are you always this lazy?" or "Are you trying to drive me nuts?"

dictator—Someone who answers definitively. The negative aspect of a dictator's response, which may necessitate further questioning, is that he may present a personal opinion as fact. He may also just have a decisive quality to responses that can be off-putting, depending on the circumstances

direct question—A question that leads with a basic interrogative.

elicitation—The technique of steering conversation toward a topic to unearth the information you want; this is not a questioning technique, but rather considered an advanced interrogation technique.

evader—Someone who tends to sidestep questions. He or she may just have an idiosyncratic way of listening and understanding rather than a desire to avoid answering. Evasion could also mean the person feels uncomfortable answering questions for some reason.

illustrator—A movement that effectively punctuates what a person is saying. It might be a finger pointing, an arm waving, a head cocked, or any number of other movements that express something about the emotion related to the statement. (Also see *batoning*.)

integrator—Someone who weighs the best way to answer your question. The person waits to hear how you respond to the answer and then may attempt to clarify the initial response, or may offer multiple answers in a single response so you know the person has considered that there may be several good answers.

leading question—A question suggesting the answer within the question; for example, "How guilty do you feel about taking that kid's lollipop?"

limbic mode—Emotions have taken over the mental state; in limbic mode a person has diminished cognitive ability.

negative question—A question that integrates negatives such as "never" or "not" so that a person is unclear about the answer. For example, "Do you ever not care about the environment?"

non-pertinent question—A question that doesn't pertain to the subject you really want to know about, but one the person will probably not lie about; it serves the purpose of seeing what the truth "looks like" and getting the person to open up to you. It also may be used to redirect attention away from a stress development or to give the questioner time to make a note or check notes.

persistent question—The same question repeated and perhaps phrased differently; it's a way to check for the thoroughness and perhaps the accuracy of the information given.

polite question—A question like "How are you?"

pre-question—A non-discovery question that asks permission to ask a question; it's often part of rapport-building.

regulator—A movement intended to control conversation, like nodding the head as if to say, "Get on with it!"

repeat question—A question that tries to uncover the same information as a previous question, but it's actually different from the first one. For example, a doctor asks you, "What time did you last have anything to eat or drink?" when you first arrive for your surgery. Just before administering anesthesia, he asks you, "You must be thirsty. How many hours has it been since you've had anything to drink?"

requestion—A non-discovery question that asks for certain responses, usually "yes" or "no," such as "Will you marry me?"

source lead—Information dropped by the respondent in the course of conversation that the questioner feels there is value in pursuing— that is, an additional person, place, thing, or event may be mentioned that warrants attention. For example, in a job interview, the candidate might thank the interviewer for holding the meeting at 9 because he's in a golf tournament that starts at noon; the interviewer would circle back to that to determine whether or not the candidate thinks that golf is more important than work.

rhetorical question—A question intended to provoke a thought, not a fact-based answer. For example, "Why do I have a conscience?"

summary question—A question that is intended to allow the person an opportunity to revisit the answer. You might *frame* the question by repeating what the person said and then ask, "How does that match up with want you want in this car?"

vague question—An indistinct question. For example, "When you went to the grocery store, did it seem like a lot of people might be just wandering around looking for something that appealed to them?"

Index

About the Authors

. . . .

James O. Pyle is a Human Intelligence Training Instructor whe has served the U.S. Army with his expertise at places such as the Defense Language Institute, the United States Army Intelligence Center and School, and the Joint Intelligence of the Pentagon. He resides in Springfield, Virginia.

Maryann Karinch is the author of 19 books, including *The Body Language Handbook*, *I Can Read You Like a Book*, and *Get People to Do What You Want*. She is the founder of The Rudy Agency, a literary agency based in Estes Park, Colorado.